praise for *FAITH*

"If you want to live a more p[...]
of fear, *FAITH* is an easy-to-[...]
why, what, and how of living [...]
Ping strikes just the right b[...]
practical aspects of bringin[...]
everyday life. *FAITH* will help you to change your life story into
one you can't wait to read."

—**DR. MARK S. ALBION**, author of
Making a Life, Making a Living
and *Leadership at Work*

"*FAITH* has a wonderfully engaging conversational style. I
read it—and I want to *meet* A. C. Ping!"

—**CYNTHIA KNEEN**, author of *Awake Mind, Open Heart*
and *Shambhala Warrior Training*

praise for *BE*

"[An] inspiring little book. . . . This book reads like a great
conversation you might have with yourself; it encourages
the reader to explore life and find those things that bring
happiness and fulfillment."

—*PUBLISHERS WEEKLY*

"This book really hits the mark. It reinforces my own belief
that if we do what excites us, in every given moment, with
joy, excitement, and integrity, we will experience the true
nature and purpose of our Being."

—**LAURA BURNS**, Gold Medalist,
Taekwondo, 2000 Olympics

A. C. PING has traveled extensively and lived and worked in the United Kingdom, Africa, and Australia.

He has been many things, including a futures trader, limo driver, teacher, scuba divemaster, tour guide, and corporate consultant.

Now he writes about new ways of living and working and assists individuals and organizations in making their bold visions become reality.

He can be found on the internet at www.insight-works.com.

ALSO BY A. C. PING

Be

Do

Sensitive Chaos
a guide to business ethics and the
creation of trust in the new millennium

The Second Coming of Capitalism
and the secret to business success
in the third millennium

FAITH

A. C. Ping

MARLOWE & COMPANY
NEW YORK

FAITH
Copyright © 2005 by A. C. Ping

Published by
Marlowe & Company
An Imprint of Avalon Publishing Group Incorporated
245 West 17th Street • 11th Floor
New York, NY 10011-5300

AVALON
publishing group incorporated

Library of Congress Cataloging-in-Publication Data
Ping, A. C., 1965–
Faith / A.C. Ping.
p. cm.
ISBN 1-56924-344-1 (pbk.)
1. Self-actualization (Psychology) I. Title.
BF637.S4P562 2005
158—dc22
2005018771

ISBN-13: 978-1-56924-344-2

9 8 7 6 5 4 3 2 1

Designed by Pauline Neuwirth, Neuwirth & Associates, Inc.
Printed in Canada

For Rosie

■

acknowledgments

Once again I am indebted to many people for the support they have given me and the positive energy that they have put into this book. In many ways the process of writing this book has indeed been a test of faith, and as always it is the people who kept believing that I am most grateful to.

You know who you are, but I know you love to see your names in print, so thanks: Jono, Lotus, Mark, Chrissie, Candice, and Jennie.

To Matthew Lore, Peter Jacoby, and all the other people at Marlowe & Company. Thanks for believing in this book and for being instrumental in taking it and the other books global. I look forward to working more with you in future and celebrating more successes.

Lastly, where would I be without Rosie, my soul mate, friend, and lover? Through the highest of highs and the lowest of lows you've not only stuck by me and held my hand, but you've continually encouraged and believed in me. You told me faith is nothing without love, and I feel blessed that you love me. Thank you.

A. C. Ping

contents

introduction

Be who you want to be, do what you want to do.

■

And then? . . . And then? . . . And then? . . .
—Chinese drive-through scene in *Dude, Where's My Car?*

if you haven't seen the movie *Dude, Where's My Car?* I guess I should explain. In a funny scene, the two main characters pull into a drive-through at a Chinese restaurant. One of them gives the order via an intercom, after which the Chinese lady at the other end asks, "And *then*?" The main character thinks for a moment, then adds a little more to the order, but the response is the same. "And *then*?" So he adds a little more, but the response is still the same. "And *then*?"

"No 'and then,'" he replies.

But she still asks, "And *then*?"

"No 'and then'!" he replies.

Still, she asks, "And *then*?"

"NO 'AND THEN'!"

"AND *THEN*?!"

"NO 'AND THEN'!"

"AND *THEN*?!"

"NO, NO, NO 'AND THEN'!"

And so it goes on until he angrily smashes the intercom in frustration.

Life can be a bit like that. You find the courage to break out of the rat race and decide to go off and be who you really want to be and do what you really want to do. Isn't that all there is to it? Surely it must be that simple. But what if what you have decided to do is REALLY BIG? What then? What if all of the people you tell your plans to look at you as if you are mad? Or what if you've decided to do something that is way, way off the mainstream? What if even the thought of it challenges you to your very core and brings up doubts and fears within you that eat away at you? What then? What do you do with all of those fears and doubts? How do you find some comfort within yourself to silence the little voice that keeps asking, "and then?" How do you find a way to release yourself from the paralysis of analysis that stops you from getting on with it?

If you're in this space, this book is for you! It is the third book in the series that began with *BE* and *DO*. It can be read on its own, but will make much more sense if you have read *BE* and *DO* first. You'll find it covers some of the areas covered in *BE* and *DO*, but this time it's from the perspective of FAITH.

How did *FAITH* come about? From the experiences that I have had following my path since *DO* was written several years ago. Like *BE* and *DO*, *FAITH* is not the be-all and end-all, but rather another attempt to share in the hope that some of the things that have helped me may help you.

When I finished writing *DO*, my publisher asked me to write another book in the series, and although I really wanted to, I truly believed at the time that that was it—BE who you want to BE, DO what you want to DO, and then NOTHING! But how wrong I was! In the years since, my journey has taken me to places that I never dreamed of, and I have found myself at times plagued by deep-seated fears and doubts about the path that I have followed. As is often the way, all along I have met people facing the same dilemmas—determined and talented people desperately pursuing their chosen life path, but still wracked from time to time with fear and doubt.

So here in one word is the answer—FAITH.

No, this isn't a religious book, although I'm sure it doesn't dishonor any religious teachings. And no, I'm not trying to convert you to some New Age way of looking at the world. What I am trying to do is share with you something that may give you comfort from the fears that taunt you to doubt your self-belief. Because beyond fear you will find a place free of anxiety and doubt where your spirit will fly like a bird that has just discovered its wings! That is how I believe we need to see the world so that we, as the collective human race, can ascend to the next level of consciousness and create a better future.

This book is divided into four parts: "Why Faith?" "Faith In What?" "Tests of Faith," and "Putting It All Together." I hope that it prompts you to think deeply and helps to release you from your inner demons. So let us begin . . .

FAITH
WHY FAITH?

seeing beyond the horizon

Faith is daring the soul to go beyond
what the eyes can see.
—J. R. R. Tolkien, *The Lord of the Rings*

what is faith? I guess we should first get some sort of grip on exactly what we are talking about here. It seems so often that people say to one another, "You've just got to have faith," but what the hell is it?

The Oxford English Dictionary defines faith as "belief in something without material or testable proof." The flipside of faith is reason—"a justification for something deduced from fact." Reason allows us to argue for things using factual evidence and when put up against faith in a rational context will win every time. But—and this is a very big but—reason confines us to what we know is possible,

3

whereas faith allows us to move beyond what the past tells us is possible. Without faith we would never create anything bold, grand, or seemingly impossible. Lack of faith leaves us as simple cogs in the economic system.

> "One can't believe impossible things."
> "I daresay you haven't had much practice," said the Queen.
> "When I was your age, I always did it for half an hour a day.
> Why, sometimes I've believed as many as six impossible
> things before breakfast."
> —LEWIS CARROLL, *Through the Looking Glass*

So faith is simply the ability to believe in something that you cannot prove. It's rather an esoteric concept, isn't it? Another one of those lofty things that people cling to so they don't have to face reality, maybe? So why would you bother to have faith in anything? Surely you would be better off to simply focus on what is right in front of you? Something you can touch, see, smell, and possibly hear? Surely it makes more sense to get a real job, make some real money, buy a real house, and live like everyone else is living. That would be much more practical than deciding that you want to be something like a poet, moviemaker, painter, or healer. "Where is the proof?" people will ask. "For what reason have you chosen to do this?"

"I have faith in my ability. I have faith in my life path," you may reply. If you have been through this situation, you may have been met with a stunned silence or a shaking of heads. You may have secretly been wishing that you could have avoided the conversation. Deep down, although you really want to have faith, you may still have nagging doubts about what you are doing. So why do you bother? Why don't you give up your delusional ideas and simply toe the line like everyone else?

> Nothing that is worth doing can be achieved in our lifetime; therefore we must be saved by hope. Nothing which is true or beautiful or good makes complete sense in any immediate context of history; therefore we must be saved by faith. Nothing we do, however virtuous, can be accomplished alone; therefore we are saved by love.
> —REINHOLD NIEBUHR, *philosopher*

Wouldn't the world be an incredibly boring place if no one could dream? As Reinhold Niebuhr points out in the above quote, faith saves us from being confined by the bounds of history. It allows us to escape from the possible and see beyond the horizon. It allows us to spread our wings and fly. But since we live in a world dominated by rational thought, one that requires some fact-based proof to justify a belief, allow me to explore another reason why faith is vitally important.

there is more to the world than the eyes can see

Without faith, our lives are a meaningless succession of unrelated happenings without rhyme or reason.
—ANONYMOUS

reason dominates our world because science has become all-powerful. As much as we would like to believe that there is more to the world than the eyes can see, this is easy to refute by someone who is against the concept. "Show me the proof," they will say.

Uh-oh! you may think at this point. Although you may know lots and lots of really good psychics, I'm sure you know none who are correct all of the time. Even the ones on TV get it wrong from time to time. In addition, there is the often used argument of, "If the psychic is so good, then why can't they tell me the lottery numbers?"—to which the

response of, "It's not ethical to do that," is usually met with roars of laughter.

And although you may believe in God and may even know someone who has experienced a miracle, once again when it comes to material proof your hands will be empty. You may be able to deduce the existence of spiritual beings, angels, or even God's hand in action, but again the requirement for factual material proof will leave you begging. Either you believe in God because you KNOW deep within yourself that it is true, or you don't.

Many of us have had experiences that we can't explain using fact-based reason. Many of us have experienced knowing who's on the phone before we answer it, having an intuitive feeling that has allowed us to avoid some sort of calamity, and many other events that we must simply attribute to the mysteries of the Universe.

It seems to me that most people reside in either one camp or the other: belief in what one experiences through the five senses, or belief that there is much more to the Universe than our five senses reveal to us. If you believe that there is more to the world than the eyes can see, you may have found yourself in situations where you have hidden this belief—maybe while at your parents' place for dinner, for example? You may also confine yourself to a group of friends who share similar beliefs so you can have conversations about "spiritual matters" without some twit constantly interrupting to tell you what an airhead you are.

Conversely, if you don't believe, then you will most likely confine yourself to the pursuit of material possessions and retain the company of people who are of the same mind-set. Sometimes these worlds collide when a non-believer has a "Road to Damascus" experience and suddenly jumps camp—much to the dismay of his or her materialistic friends, who quickly and selfishly give up on him or her and instead try to convince him or her to give them all of the fantastic material possessions that they will no longer need in their newfound life. But I digress . . .

In any case, what if you could link the spiritual and material worlds together? How dramatically would that change the world?

Recent scientific research is beginning to provide just such a linkage, and it has huge implications for how we see the world and our place in it.

There is an increasing amount of scientific research coming out to support the notion that the world consists of much more than the eyes can see. Most of it is in the field of physics and involves the inability of that science to reconcile the very large with the very small in order to create a theory of everything—a unifying theory. What I mean is that scientists have been confused by the fact that theories that explain the interactions of very large objects, like galaxies and the formation of the Universe, often seem to fail when they are applied to small objects such as subatomic particles. The most likely unifying theory is something called string theory, which is pointing to the existence of multiple universes! There is also a wealth of more basic science that refutes the idea that the world simply is as we experience it with the five basic senses. Thus even the most rational of our creations—science—cannot explain our world! What we are beginning to realize, from a rational scientific perspective, is that we don't know how the world works. Given this failing of science, we need to continuously use faith to move our understanding forward.

A little while ago I came across an amazing book by Dr. Rupert Sheldrake called *The Sense of Being Stared At and Other Unexplained Powers of the Human Mind* (Three Rivers Press, 2003). The first thing I did when I found the book was wonder what this guy was a doctor of and whether or not he had any credibility in the scientific community at all. To my surprise, I found that he is in fact very well respected in the scientific community, and one of his books, *Dogs That Know When Their Owners Are Coming Home* (Three Rivers Press, 2000), was actually awarded a prize for being the best science book in the United Kingdom. He is also, understandably, a controversial figure.

Anyway, in *The Sense of Being Stared At*, Dr. Sheldrake examines the evidence for whether or not the mind actually extends out beyond the physical body through things like extrasensory perception (ESP) and precognition. For example, can we tell whether or not we are being stared at by someone else without looking to check? Most people have had an experience where they have been walking down the street or having a drink in a bar when, without thinking, they turn and lock eyes with someone who has been staring at them. In most cases we put this down to pure coincidence, but what Dr. Sheldrake set out to test was whether or not people could actually "sense" being stared at.

I won't go into exactly how he and his team went about it, but suffice to say they used proper scientific methods and appropriate controls. The results of their studies are astounding. They found that YES people *can* tell when they are being stared at—some with up to 90 percent accuracy. And YES there *is* evidence to support the fact that we can influence others without physically interacting with them.

The conclusion that Sheldrake comes to in the book is even more astounding. He says that there is a hitherto unnamed field of energy that links us all together and that we are all able to "tap into" this field to varying degrees. He calls this field the "morphic field."

What, then, are the implications of this conclusion?

Well, they are huge! They take a lot of the assumptions that most of us make about the world and turn them on their heads. The physical distance between ourselves becomes much more irrelevant. Feelings and intentions take on a much larger role in the world. And guess what? Faith suddenly becomes a not so lofty concept.

Why? Because if we are all interlinked by this morphic field and the energy that we put out into the world influences

others, then our beliefs and intentions become much more powerful than we previously imagined.

As I wrote in *BE*, Descartes had it wrong when he said *"cognito ergo sum"*—"I think, therefore I am." Instead I think it should be, "I believe, therefore I am." What you believe in is key, and the faith to believe in something that has no material proof becomes extremely important.

But that still leaves us with the question of why psychics can't get it right all of the time . . .

a gigantic shimmer of huge potential

If you will it,
it is not a dream.
—THEODORE HERZL

if you believe in fate or destiny, then you will believe that your future is already determined—that it is fixed and there is nothing much you can do about it. If this were the case, then a good psychic would be able to tap into the morphic field and tell you exactly what was going to happen to you in the future. However, as I wrote in *BE*, this would mean that there would be no point at all in trying to change anything in your life or in trying to influence the course of the world. No matter what you did, things would still turn out the same and all of your efforts would be in vain.

I reject this concept because I believe that it confines us to the status of rats in a cage. In turn this would make God or any other higher force or creative power in the Universe very cruel. Before we have even begun, our most basic right—the right to choose how to influence our lives—would be taken away from us.

Instead, what I believe is that the world is a gigantic shimmer of huge potential in which all possible futures exist at the same time—a bit like string theory. In this view of the world we have a continuous opportunity in the present to influence not only our own futures, but also the collective future of all of us.

How does this work? Think about it from the morphic field perspective. If there is a field that links us all together and we can both tap into it and influence it by the energy we put out there, then we become cocreators in the Universe. Note that we are not sole creators—although I'm sure it is an appealing concept to be a God-like figure. We need to take into account the collective intentions of the rest of the human race and also the influence of God or any other higher power.

As cocreators in the Universe, we have a direct influence on the future. Our intentions combined with our beliefs create our world. Having clear intentions and beliefs will increase our chances of being able to create exactly what we want.

But where does faith come into this?

Well, if we are only able to believe in what we know to be possible because of reason and justifiable by fact, then we will be bound by history. In other words, we will not be able to see beyond the horizon or create anything bold, grand, or seemingly impossible.

Faith allows us to change our world via proactive intent. Without it there is no hope for a future other than what we believe to be possible based on the past.

we are all emotional, not rational

What we have done for ourselves alone dies with us.
What we have done for others and the world remains
and is immortal.
—ALBERT PINE

are you with me so far? I know this is all a bit technical and in the head, but what I'm trying to present to you here is a more rational argument for something that is an esoteric concept. I hope you can bear with me, as I think it is important to present to you a reason-based argument so that the rational side of your mind can understand why faith is important. Otherwise when you are confronted with purely rational fears and doubts, you will have nothing to refute those fears other than what could be called lofty concepts.

Anyway, let's have a look at what's wrong with the current system that dominates the world today—free market economics. Boring, yes I know, but again please bear with me . . .

Free market economics is based on the assumption that we are all rational beings. That if we are faced with a choice between one brand of widget costing one dollar versus another brand costing two dollars, we will choose the cheaper one.

However, philosophers have coined the term "rational fool" to describe the person who makes short-term decisions for their own benefit without taking into account the long-term implications of those decisions. I think that in the Western world we have become masters of creating rational fools.

Free market economics is a beautiful theory that makes perfect sense when viewed through idealistic eyes. Why wouldn't we want to support a system that gives all of us the ability to choose from a variety of different products all delivered to us at the best possible prices? To be free to work for whomever we want at the highest negotiated wages and to be free to invest in whatever we want? Freedom and equality—that's what it's all about, and who could possibly argue with it?

Hmmm . . . Great idea, but let's look at the reality. Am I being cynical if I suggest that the real values driving our society, now that free market philosophy is at its heart, are greed and fear?

I know, I know, it's an outrageous suggestion, but consider the facts. We are all little pawns in the free market system, desperately trying to look after ourselves while competing against everyone else. Take the example of layoffs—we are all trying to outdo each other so we don't lose our jobs. Or promotions—we are all trying to get ahead on the corporate ladder, make more money, and have more assets.

Why? Money talks. The more money you have, the more you can protect yourself from the nasty elements of society. You can drive a car to work instead of catching the bus; you can have private health insurance instead of having to depend on Medicaid or get by with no coverage at all; you can live in a place that has security entrances; and so on. The more money you have, the more opportunities you can create for yourself and your offspring—you can afford to join private clubs where you can meet people who make good business contacts or who give you little snippets of inside information. You can send your children to private schools, buy them a place in college, afford to send them overseas for exposure to other cultures, and eventually get them a job in a corporation run by one of the people you've met at your private club.

That's all fair, isn't it?

I don't know. I think it's more like the line in the movie *Wall Street*—"You're either on the inside or on the outside. There's nothing in between."

The problem is that we all know that there's nothing in between, so we all fear that we could be left on the outside. We'd really like to be able to care about the people who are left on the outside, but we're too busy trying to make sure that we stay on the inside. Ho hum . . . If only we could live in the world of *Star Trek*, where there are unlimited resources and no need for a system of uneven competitive distribution.

Because of our fears we are happy to do the things that intuitively we wouldn't want to have done to us. We lay people off, push people to work harder, and cut as many corners as we can so the company we work for can make as much money as possible so that we can keep our jobs and maybe even get a pay raise. We are always chasing that dangling carrot.

Along the way we are bombarded by all manner of messages that reinforce the fact that we need to have more things. Because, let's face it, if you're working your ass off for some corporation, then you need to have something to provide you with a sense that you really are successful. Things like new cars, big houses, and lots of the latest cool trinkets and gadgets. Every day we see hundreds of advertisements showing us how happy we could be if we could just have a big-screen TV, a new BMW, some nice new clothes, and maybe even a cell phone that takes pictures.

So what is the effect of all of this, and what has this got to do with faith?

Well, instead of being rational, our emotions drive us. Unfortunately, fear and greed dominate the world, and they are the emotions that start to control us. We fear that if someone else has more, then we will have less. We fear that if we don't look after ourselves, then no one else will. Greed drives us to have more and more and more . . .

The result? Are we now afraid of each other? If someone starts to talk to you on a train do you become suspicious of their motives? If someone makes eye contact with you as you pass them in the street do you greet them or look away?

If we are afraid of each other, then what sort of world are we creating via our collective beliefs?

do you have protection?

in our rational society dominated by fear, greed, and suspicion of one another, we are bound to get hurt. As emotional beings, the experience of being in the world can be very painful.

Given this pain, most of us decide that we need some sort of protection. We ask ourselves if we can trust other people and ultimately whether or not human nature is good or bad.

Now, from a fact-based "reason" perspective, we look at the world and the negative images that are presented to us on a daily basis via the media and very logically deduce that the evidence shows humans to be bad.

The protection that most of us choose is cynicism. We begin to doubt the motives of those around us, and instead of taking things at face value, we begin to look for other alternatives. For example, we see a news report showing a businessman donating millions of dollars to a third world country, but instead of applauding his philanthropy we ask what material benefit it is that he might be getting out of the deal.

But where does this leave us? If we constantly doubt the motives of those around us, then we put this "feeling" or judgment out into the world, and in turn we play a role in creating this negative perception of human nature. This creates more proof that our judgment of human nature as being bad is correct and, yes, you guessed it, we go around and around the loop—a nasty loop that leaves us fearful of how people will react if we decide to go after our dreams . . .

The alternative? Faith in human nature and hope that we can create a better world. But where is the evidence? It's much easier to be fearful than to believe in something that has little or no supporting evidence.

Our fears stop us from taking the leap, but that just means we go around and around again . . .

the power of our story

If we continue down the same path we have chosen,
then the danger is we will end up where we are headed.
—CHINESE PROVERB

as human beings we need to make sense of the world. The way we do this is by assembling in our minds a story about the world that explains, or justifies, events as they happen.

It's simply the way we are hardwired. If we didn't have a story, then we'd have to spend our entire lives slowly going through every single situation that we came across and weighing the pros and cons of different options. The story that we tell ourselves allows us to make quick judgments about different situations without necessarily having to go through all of the background or evidence behind them.

The problem is that the story that we tell ourselves is all-powerful. It creates our world via our beliefs and intentions. If the story that we tell ourselves is that humans are essentially bad and we have adopted a cynical approach to life to protect ourselves emotionally, then guess what? We create it . . .

So what to do? Well, we need to change the story, don't we?

But how do we change the story when we are being bombarded on a daily basis with so much negative evidence to prove that mankind does bad things and that there are evil people out there in the world?

Most of us sit back and wait for people to prove to us that they are in fact good before we will shift from our cynical position and give something back in return. But where does that leave us? Once again we are in a reactive cycle where we have effectively given up on our ability to proactively take responsibility and put something positive into the world. Remember the morphic field? Well, this position leaves us as part of the problem rather than the solution.

But if I put myself out there I may get hurt! I hear you cry. And that's the point. What exactly are you waiting for? Proof?

You need to change your story without having proof. That is where faith comes into the picture . . .

conscious evolution?

The great revolutions of history have not changed the world,
they have changed man.
—Eric Hiller

as human beings we are in a unique situation—we
are the only creatures on the planet that can choose to consciously evolve. We can choose to continue to tell the story
that human nature is bad, that fear and greed permeate the
world, and that we need to protect ourselves from others,
OR we can stop being reactive to events, make a conscious
choice to regain our power as cocreators in the Universe,
and proactively create a better world.

We need to believe in something beyond what factual
evidence presents to us. We need to find a way of remembering just how powerful we really are and how we truly

can change the planet just through a conscious shift in our beliefs.

Without faith we confine ourselves to continuing to live in a world dominated by fear and greed. Without faith we cling desperately to the cloak of cynicism to protect ourselves from being hurt by others. And most importantly, without faith we undermine our own ability to really get onto our life path and BE who we want to BE and DO what we want to DO. Instead, we put ourselves in a situation where our own fears and doubts consume our passions and kill our dreams.

So are you prepared to jump? Come on a journey with me and I will show you how . . .

FAITH IN WHAT?

faith that life has meaning

The life committed to nothing larger than itself
is a meager life indeed.
—Martin E. P. Seligman

SO what should we have faith in? The first step is to embrace the fact that life has meaning. Why? Well, let's look at it from the opposite point of view—what if you decide to be a nihilist and believe in nothing at all? If you believe in nothing, then the only thing that you are left with are the events that arise on a daily basis. In this scenario you are ruled by circumstance and your emotions. If something bad happens to you, then there is no deeper meaning in it—it is simply a bad event. You have no ability to see any deeper reason for it other than it is simply bad—you have no choice but to experience the emotions that arise in you as a reaction to the event. You cannot learn from the event other than possibly trying to control or suppress your emotions. You cannot find any comfort in the event by saying something like, *I don't know why this is happening to me but I trust there is a reason*. No, you must just accept it and react. Likewise, if something good happens to you, then you can embrace the emotions that arise in you as a reaction to the event.

If you believe in nothing, then you must just bumble along accepting events and circumstances as they arise. Life simply has no deeper meaning than what appears at the surface level. But—yes, unfortunately there is a but— you still get hurt by negative events that leave you with your negative emotions. So, like all of us, you still need protection. If you believe in nothing, then your choice of protection will most likely be cynicism. You will take a sarcastic view of the world and be ruled by feelings of jealousy if you see others experiencing better things in life than you. You will take no responsibility for the events of your life, and in turn you will give up any power that you have to change things. In addition, you will find that you take no responsibility for your influence on other people. If you are in a bad mood, then you are simply in a bad mood and other people will just have to cope with it—too bad for them. . . . Life just *is*, remember? There's no deeper meaning in events than what you can see. You are simply a passenger. Events will dictate your mood, rather than the other way around. The only escape will be hedonistic pleasure, and that will only last as long as the hedonistic event lasts—you will always be searching for more . . .

Is this you? If it is, I ask you to consider how much of your power you are giving up by taking this position.

What if you believe in no higher power or creative force in the Universe, but you still believe in doing good things in the world or in treating people the way you would like to be treated? Are you doing these good things because you believe that if you treat people well, you are more likely to be treated well yourself? If so, you are effectively saying that you believe in the notion of karma—or that what goes around comes around.

If that's the case, then guess what? You are by implication saying that you believe in the existence of an unseen higher power or force that is keeping some sort of tally of good and bad events and redistributing the energy to the ones doing the events. You are saying that there is meaning in events.

But does faith that life has meaning necessarily mean that you have to believe in God? This is something that I have found stops people in their tracks when they start to delve into a spiritual path in life. As I said earlier, people either believe in God or they don't. Many people have had early life experiences that have made them rebel against structured religions, and for most this leaves them struggling with how to make sense of the Universe. Some decide to believe in nothing—the nihilists—but this leaves them in the precarious position of being ruled by circumstances and their emotions, the result of which we've already discussed.

So can we separate faith from religion? I believe that we can. It isn't necessary to believe in God to be able to believe that there is meaning in life. Now, don't get me wrong here—I'm not saying there is no God—That is up to you to decide for yourself. What I'm saying is that if you are going to put yourself out there and try to be who you want to be and do what you want to do, then you need to be able to find some comfort and meaning in events as they happen—beyond just the surface issues.

You simply need to have faith that there is some meaning in life. I'm not saying I know what that meaning is—and this is where spirituality and religion diverge. Religions tend to give you the answers, whereas a spiritual path will simply give you the questions and you have to figure out the answers.

I believe that life is a mystery and that we should never stop trying to understand it, but we should also never expect to be able to fully comprehend it. From a religious perspective this would mean that we should never expect to be able to comprehend the workings of God's mind, as he is just too vast and powerful for us to fully understand.

Let me just summarize here before your head explodes: If we are to find some comfort from our fears and doubts as we step into the void and attempt to pursue our dreams, then we must have faith that there is some meaning in life and the events of our lives. I don't know what that meaning is—I can guess and propose some answers, but I can never know for sure. I believe that we all need to ask and attempt to answer that question for ourselves.

We need to have faith in our ability to influence the world and not resign ourselves to fate. We are not pawns, but we are also not in complete control. We are cocreators, not sole creators.

If you can find faith that life has meaning, then you will be able to more readily accept unfavorable events as they happen and consciously learn and grow from them. If you have faith, then you can embrace your own power and take some responsibility for how you are being in the world and what you are helping to create in the world.

Oh yes, and one final thing—I cannot offer you any proof that life has meaning. I can only ask you to have faith that it does.

faith in one's self

Our deepest fear is not that we are inadequate.
Our deepest fear is that we are powerful beyond measure.
It is our light, not our darkness that most frightens us.
We ask ourselves, Who am I to be brilliant, gorgeous,
talented, and fabulous?
Actually, who are you *not* to be?
You are a child of God.
Your playing small doesn't serve the world.
There's nothing enlightened about shrinking
so that other people won't feel insecure around you.
We are all meant to shine, as children do.
We are born to manifest the glory of God that is within us.
It's not just in some of us; it's in everyone.
And as we let our light shine, we unconsciously give
other people permission to do the same.
As we're liberated from our own fear,
our presence automatically liberates others.
—MARIANNE WILLIAMSON, *A Return to Love*

if you believe that life has meaning and you also acknowledge that we are not simply pawns in the game of life, then you will also need to acknowledge that YOU have a huge responsibility.

Yes, YOU! Little old you, sitting there reading this, are playing a role in creating the world as we know it. YOU have just as much power to influence the world as anyone else. The trick is acknowledging and accepting that power.

Scary thought, isn't it? But as Marianne Williamson pointed out, shrinking from this responsibility and playing small doesn't serve the world. Yes, it may be easier to sit back, watch other people create the world, and then bitch about what a shitty job they are doing, but where does that leave you?

If you really want to get out there and follow your dreams, then you need to step up to the plate. You need to change your internal story, take responsibility, and embrace your divine nature.

Great sports figures often provide us with the best demonstration of what this means in practice. One shining example of such a person is the late, great Ayrton Senna. If you are unfamiliar with him, Ayrton Senna was a Formula One race car driver whose life was tragically cut short in 1994. While he was alive, Senna continually pushed back the boundaries of what people thought it was possible to do in a Formula One car. In an interview in 1989, Senna provided insight into what can happen when you embrace your light and change your internal story. Here is part of what he said:

> I still don't know how far I can go. It is all a learning process, something I work very hard to keep clear in my mind. I aim to have a really realistic, clear understanding of what is going on, and what I am doing—and what I can do. I can only try what I believe I can do, but by trying I often find I can do more. Then I have to readjust.
>
> Every time I have an idea about where my limits are, I go to check it and most of the time I am wrong. So I have to adjust myself to going even further. It is very exciting and it is a non-stop process.

What story do you tell yourself about what you are capable of? Are you brave enough to live your own legend? To go on the journey that your soul has chosen for you in this lifetime?

Faith that you truly are a being of infinite potential is what you need to do this. But again, I can't give you any proof . . .

faith in others and the nature of oneness

I can never be what I ought to be
until you are what you ought to be,
and you can never be what you ought to be
until I am what I ought to be.
This is the inter-related structure of reality.
—MARTIN LUTHER KING JR.

there is an absolute truth to which all spiritual and religious teachings refer. It is a truth that our current rational society seems to deny, but it is something that individually we cannot deny.

We are all interlinked. There is truly only one life. WE ARE ONE.

As I discussed earlier, the discovery of the morphic field using a scientific method provides some proof for this truth, but it can be a challenging truth to accept nonetheless. If we are all ONE, then that means we are not simply inter-linked with all of the people who we admire or aspire to be; we are also interlinked with people such as Adolf Hitler, Pol Pot, and Idi Amin. If the thought that you are truly a power-ful being scares you, then this truth probably scares you even more, but denying it is to delude one's self about the true nature of existence.

Denying that we are all ONE will stop you from ascend-ing to your true and full potential. Acceptance of it may mean that you have to dramatically change your internal story about how the world works and your role in it.

Consider the implications. If we are all interlinked and all ONE, then:

- Distance is irrelevant to how we influence each other.

- My happiness is your happiness.

- My pain is your pain.

- My fear is your fear.

You get back from the world what you put into the world.

So long as you are holding someone down, some part of you must be down there with them. You aren't serving yourself by being selfish, fearful, or greedy; you are harm-ing yourself.

FAITH

But what about all the horrible people in the world? I hear you scream. What about all of the EVIDENCE?

I'm sure you know the answer—FAITH . . .

I never said this was going to be an easy one, did I?

To have faith in others and the true nature of oneness means that we need to be able to have faith in the highest potential of human nature and in the ability of human beings to transcend themselves.

This, I believe, is at least part of the story of judgment day as referred to in various religious teachings. DO YOU HAVE FAITH IN HUMAN NATURE?

If you don't, then guess what? You will fear others, you will be greedy and selfish, and YOU will actively play a part in creating a greedy, selfish world.

Letting it go is difficult, I know, but the other choice is even more frightening.

Once again, there is little or no proof for this . . .

TESTS OF FAITH

> Of all the creatures of earth,
> only human beings can change their patterns.
> Man alone is the architect of his destiny.
> —WILLIAM JAMES

I guess by now you may be thinking that you get it, but all of this is simply too hard. I can relate to where you are at. I've been there. I've tried and failed and then tried to deny it all. I've given up, gone and put my head back in the sand. But then something weird has always happened. I've found that I couldn't deny the essential truth in these teachings if I truly wanted to follow the path in life that I laid out in *BE* and *DO*.

I found that without faith life has no meaning; without faith in myself, and without faith in others, I had no really

good way of dealing with all of my fears and doubts. I could strive to do amazing things, but then out of the blue bad things would happen to me. Unless I had faith that there was indeed a reason behind them, I couldn't cope. I could be a "good" and caring person, but then "bad" people would come my way and knock me down. Without faith in others I found myself on a lonely island. Finally, when I was right out there with everything I had on the line, I found that if I didn't have faith in myself there really was no one else who could give it to me.

So how do you do it? How do you face the seemingly harsh events that test your faith to the core?

This section of the book is solely devoted to tests of faith. It looks first at faith itself and then goes through some of the tests you may face in the three different areas that I outlined in the previous section—"faith that life has meaning," "faith in one's self," and "faith in others and the nature of oneness." I hope that some or all of the ideas here will help you when you find yourself doubting the very validity of your beliefs.

finding faith

To really become free inside
takes either courage or disaster . . .
I recommend courage.
—CHRISTOPHER REEVE

how do you find faith if you have none? It's very easy to say things like, "Take a deep breath and jump!" but what does that actually mean? How do you jump when all of the factual evidence says it's a crazy and delusional thing to do?

In the first part of this book I presented a reason-based argument for why you should have faith, but then reason can only carry us so far before we must leap.

I think at the end of the day what we need to acknowledge is that belief is all we have. We believe, therefore we are. Your beliefs create your reality. If you don't believe that you are a powerful being, then you aren't. If you don't believe that there is meaning in life, then most likely you will find that there isn't. If you don't believe human nature is essentially good, then you will find evidence to support that belief.

The key to all of this is that we are always true to our perceptions. If we perceive that things are a certain way, then we will act accordingly, and by acting accordingly we create that reality.

It's another one of those nasty little loops, isn't it? But who traps you in it?

YOU.

You can analyze this forever, but at some point you will need to drop your fears and make a choice. Jump or not?

I can't make you jump—no one can. You need to do it yourself, and no amount of rational argument or reasoning will get you there.

A friend of mine found herself in this situation. Her life was miserable. She felt that life had dealt her a poor hand of cards. Her parents had died in quick succession of each other, and even though they had left her financially well-off, all she could see was that she had been abandoned by them. Boyfriends came and went, but none stuck around. Work in her chosen field eluded her. She found herself getting older and without a partner while her friends were getting married and having children.

She became jaded and cynical. She kept looking for things to get better, but all she got was more of the same.

As she became more cynical about life, her friends found her increasingly difficult to be around. Although I'm sure she felt that she was fun to be around as she partied up a storm, most people found her sarcasm and cynicism hard to bear, so many stopped seeing her.

Finally, she found out that she couldn't have children. The most basic reason for living, the need to reproduce, had been denied to her. She found herself with a stark choice—let go of her cynical view of the world or find some faith.

She jumped—suddenly many things began to make sense to her. Her newfound faith in life made her easier to be around. She started taking responsibility for how she was being. Friends came back to her side; new boyfriends appeared. Life took on a whole new feeling.

Do you know people like this?

> Only when it is dark enough can you see the stars.
> —Martin Luther King Jr

Our fears can rule us and dominate our lives. When things are going along well it is easy to just take it as it comes, but when things start to go bad we need something else to help us through the hard times. How many people do you know who suddenly start praying when they are in a tough situation?

Do you want to wait until your life is overrun by fear before you make a decision to jump?

We can wait and wonder and analyze as much as we want, but the truth is that we, individually, are the only ones who can make the decision to take a leap of faith.

So maybe that's not much comfort, but that's reality. It's as simple as making a firm decision and then living it—BEING it!

blind faith

Doubt is uncomfortable, certainty is ridiculous.
—Voltaire

must we adopt our position of faith and then never question it? Am I proposing that once you leap there will be no lapses of faith?

Far from it! Blind and unquestioning faith will make you blind. It was blind faith in the leadership and ideas of people like Hitler that led to unimaginable atrocities being perpetrated against other human beings. It is blind faith in various fundamentalist religious teachings that is contributing to many of the problems now facing the world.

We are all individually powerful human beings. Part of that power is our ability to question our faith, not only in ourselves, but in the beliefs of others as well.

FAITH

Lapses of faith are opportunities to look at the world anew. By constantly questioning our faith we are constantly renewing it. This also applies to faith in ourselves.

Once you decide that you will break the shackles of normality and pursue what you are really passionate about in life, you may believe that all will be rosy. The truth is that if you are right out there taking a big leap, you will find that you fall down even more regularly than you did before. Each time you fall, however, you will be faced with a choice—either turn back, or gather your strength, renew your faith in yourself, and get back on track.

At the same time, an amazing thing will happen—every time you are faced with a crisis or test of faith and get yourself through it, you will find that you are stronger and more able to face the challenges ahead. This is the way the world works.

What you need to trust is that you will not be given challenges that you are not up to. This is where faith in the meaning of life comes in, and this is where each challenge will give you an opportunity to learn something new that you will need for the next step of your journey.

I know this sounds contrite, but looked at in this way, even the greatest and most arduous tests of faith should be seen as welcome opportunities to grow. Although none of us like change, it is often when we are most uncomfortable that we have the best chance to find the strength and courage that we need to fulfill our dreams.

FAITH

So take a deep breath, accept that faith implies uncertainty, and embrace the tests that come your way. For without them you are sure to be stuck in a situation that may even leave you blind.

faith that life has meaning

the deadly deal

Unbidden seeds of regret
born on malicious backs
Bloom in weary kingdoms.
—ANONYMOUS

there is a deal that many of us try to make with life. It goes something like this—*If I behave myself and am "good," then will you (life) look after me and make sure that nothing bad will happen to me?*

Guess what? WRONG . . .

You can't make a deal with life. Yes, the rule of karma does eventually hold, but just because you are always doing good things and denying your dark side doesn't mean that nothing bad will ever happen to you. Bad things happen to good people—that is a simple fact of life. Why is this so?

Surely that is simply unfair. But who ever said life was fair?

When historian Charles A. Beard was asked what he had learned from History, he answered,

> First, whom the gods would destroy
> they must first make mad with power.
> Second, the mills of God grind slowly,
> yet they grind exceedingly small.
> Third, the bee fertilizes the flower it robs.
> Fourth, when it is dark enough you can see the stars.

Having faith that life has meaning doesn't mean that you selectively have faith. It means that you have to embrace the good with the bad and be willing to let go of the need to control life in some way.

The workings of the world are a mystery, remember? Having faith that there is meaning doesn't necessarily mean you will be able to understand what that meaning is. Often you will find with the passing of time that the meaning of past events will be revealed to you, but don't think you will be saved by some of the unpleasant things in life by attempting to make some deal. To do so is to set yourself up for "unbidden seeds of regret."

past the point of no return

a funny thing may happen to you on the road of life that won't seem so funny at the time. Once you decide that you are going to throw off the shackles of conformity and go off and pursue your dreams, you may find that initially everything goes along extremely easily. People suddenly come into your life and give you the help that you need. Finances fall into place. Providence moves with you.

Until . . . you pass the point of no return. Then, oh yes, those doubts that you had neatly packed away in a little box burst forth and rear their ugly heads. As you sit on the plane on the way to Africa to work as a volunteer aid worker, having quit your high-paying job and sold all of your possessions, you find yourself wracked with doubt. *What sort of a nutcase am I?* you may ask. *Am I insane? I had a great job, with fantastic career prospects; I was only six months away*

from a promotion; my car was almost paid off . . . WHAT AM I DOING?

It's easy to be brave when we know we have an "out." *Oh yes, I'm committed to this path,* you say to yourself— but secretly, quietly, in the deep recesses of your mind, a little voice will be saying, *Don't worry, I've got it covered; you can still get out of it.*

Ho hum . . .

Alex was in his mid-thirties. He'd had a failed marriage in his twenties and had spent the majority of the years since taking courses, dealing with his "shit," and getting it togeth-er so he could go off and have the sort of loving, caring rela-tionship that he really wanted. Then he met Sarah. He was committed, or so he said. Time passed by, she moved in, and he kept repeating that he was committed—until she came to him one morning and said she was pregnant. Instead of being happy, Alex FREAKED OUT! The "out" option had disappeared.

What to do? Just accept that this may happen to you AND that it happens to most people. Your faith will be test-ed on whatever path you choose. Why does it happen just when you pass the point of no return?

Well, how can it be truly tested while you still have an "out"?

In these times you will need to take yourself off to some-where quiet, allow your fears and doubts to surface, and then face them one by one. Yes, you can still run, but where will that get you if this is what you REALLY want to do? Remember that YOU are the one who chose to go down this path—no one forced you to do it!

Take comfort in the fact that this "test" doesn't just happen to you. Seek out someone you respect to talk with. Everyone has doubts from time to time—it's what you do with them that matters.

If you really want to live your life's dream, then at some point you have to DO it.

For years, I've wanted to start a retreat center. At one point I thought I'd found the perfect place in Far North Queensland, Australia. As I made preparations for the great shift in my life, many things fell neatly into place. I got a consulting contract that allowed me to have enough money so I could take the needed time off to find the right property. Everyone I told about the idea thought it was fantastic—many pledged support to send groups of people there. I had a great drive up there—everything seemed to be on track.

But then I got there and the wheels started to fall off. The money started to run out. I couldn't do the sort of work I'd been used to doing. I started to get desperate. The only work available was what I considered, in my esteemed frame of mind, to be below me.

Because I didn't have a simple "out," the only option seemed to be to pack the whole thing in. At the end of my tether, I spoke with my brother about it—and he said something that has stuck with me ever since. "Sure," he said.

"You can pack it all in, give up on your dreams, put your tail between your legs, and go and get a 'real' job, but then what's going to happen? As soon as you get comfortable are you going to try to do all of this again?"

Oh shit! That helped me put everything into perspective.

If not now, then when?

When you find yourself past the point of no return and your doubts resurface, ask yourself that question—if you give up now, will you just want to do it all over again later on?

If the answer is yes, then you must take a deep breath and hold the course. You may still not get what you expect, but at least as you test your faith you will find that it gets stronger and prepares you for what is to come.

nothing's happening— or is it?

As you set out for Ithaka
hope your road is a long one . . .
And if you find her poor, Ithaka won't have fooled you.
Wise as you will have become, so full of experience,
you'll have understood by then what these Ithakas mean.
—CONSTANTINE P. CAVAFY, Greek poet

one of the most frustrating times along the path of life occurs when NOTHING seems to be happening. Even the times when bad things are happening can be easier to deal with than the times when absolutely NOTHING is shifting. When bad stuff is happening at least you can address it, and even if you are struggling, you are generally so consumed with just trying to keep your head above the water that you simply don't have too much time to think.

But when NOTHING is happening, oh how frustrating that can be! Not only do you have lots of time to think, but at the same time lots of people keep asking you what is happening, which of course only serves to make things worse!

A friend of mine finished his PhD recently. He'd worked extremely hard to get it, and it was in what seemed to be a very relevant field with regard to the events of the day. Along the path of achieving the degree he'd faced many challenges—people had doubted him; he'd doubted himself. While he'd battled away for years living on a paltry income, many of his friends had pursued careers that didn't require years of education and had now bought houses and achieved some measure of material success.

When the thesis was finally submitted he figured that he would now be on easy street. A good job would come, respect from his peers would come with the new title of Doctor, and his life would change. To say that he was brash and arrogant about his newfound status in life would be an understatement.

But how wrong he was! Despite having numerous written endorsements from well-known and respected academics, no matter how many job applications he submitted, none delivered to him his new life.

As the months ticked by, his confidence wavered. The more often people asked whether he had a job, the more he began to lose hope. Eventually he stopped talking about it; questions about jobs were waved away with a brush of the hand. Nothing seemed to be happening.

But of course, that was on the surface. Underneath, a great shift was occurring. His arrogance was being replaced with humility. Instead of having a fixed opinion on every topic, he began to listen. Instead of demanding, he started giving.

Sometimes when we climb great mountains that take all of our energy and effort, we believe that when we get to the top we will find salvation. We focus on the end point and forget two things: first, that the journey may be more valuable than just getting to the end point; and second, that the end point may in fact not be the end point at all.

The first peak that you reach may not be the highest peak at all. When you get to the top you may find yourself sitting on a plateau blinded by the mist. As you grope around in the darkness trying to find your way you may become frustrated. But instead of becoming frustrated, it may just be that life is giving you a safe place to rest and gather your energy for the journey ahead. You may not be able to see which way to go, but if you sit patiently, have faith that life has meaning, and wait until the mist clears, you may find that one day you wake up to a bright blue sky that reveals a clear path leading up an even more beautiful mountain than the one you have just climbed.

I know this is not easy. The temptation will be to run around in the mist searching and searching for guidance. But all this will do is wear you out, and in turn the mist will

remain firmly in place until you stop and rest. No further path will be revealed to you until you have the energy to attempt the next climb.

> Everyone is in the best seat.
> —JOHN CAGE

In these times of frustration, have faith. Trust that when the time is right, it will happen. Trust that although nothing seems to be happening on the surface, a whole lot is happening below the surface. Just because you can't see it doesn't mean it is not there.

spirit knows the
fastest way

Give to the world the best that you have,
and the best will come back to you.
—MADELINE BRIDGES

if you are a control freak like me, you may have already worked out your ideal Vision and decided all by yourself EXACTLY how you are going to get there. You may have specific goals for when you are going to achieve each point along the journey. You may even have things worked out week-by-week in a fixed schedule that tells you what, how, and when you will be doing specific things.

Do you really think you can dictate your life like that? Do you really think you can tell the universal spirit or God when and how things will happen?

I mean seriously, get a grip here!

FAITH

In *DO* I talked about working out a ladder to the future and determining what the milestones are along the way. I'm not now saying that you should throw the ladder away, or that you can't have specific goals. Rather, what I am saying is that you need to let go of the inflexibility around it.

When you decide to pursue a spiritual path in life, you need to accept that the workings of the Universe are much more complex than you can ever comprehend. Once you take the time to clarify what your Vision is—as I outlined in *BE*—and you have put in the effort to manifest that on a "feeling" plane—as outlined in *DO*—then you need to let it go.

Let it go? Yes! Have clarity with your Vision—what does it look like, smell like, sound like, and most importantly FEEL like? Stand there in your ideal future. What is the FEELING that you have? FEELINGS are the language of creation. If you know what it FEELS like, you can set your intention with absolute clarity and CALL that future into this material plane.

Once you have put your FEELING via INTENTION out there into the Universe—let go of it and BE PRESENT to what is happening right here in front of you. Holding on to your Vision and what you think is the fastest path to it will only leave you with frustration. What makes you think that the course that YOU have decided is the best and fastest one?

As I wrote earlier, I once wanted to set up a retreat center. Although many years ago I had found myself—via serendipity—living on a beautiful farm at the base of the

Drakensberg Mountains in South Africa, which I knew deep in my heart would be *the* best place for a retreat center, I had decided that it was an impossible dream and had instead found myself trying to set it up closer to home in far north Australia. I had decided that this was the best, most practical way to achieve my goal.

When the idea for the retreat center in Australia failed, I was incredibly frustrated. *SPIRIT KNOWS THE FASTEST WAY*, I tried to keep telling myself, even though I was incredibly annoyed by what had happened and was vigorously trying to work out the best way—using my rational mind—to get myself back on track.

Well, guess where I am now? Yep—living on the farm at the base of the mountains in Africa . . .

> The gaps are the thing. The gaps are the
> spirit's one home, the altitudes and latitudes
> so dazzlingly spare and clean that the spirit
> can discover itself like a once blind man unbound.
> —ANNIE DILLARD

I could NEVER have worked that path out for myself, but in retrospect it makes perfect sense—my experience allowed me to learn many of the things that I needed to get to where I am now.

Along my path I've spoken to many other people who have experienced the same kind of thing, and it all comes down to trusting and having faith that there are reasons for

events as they happen—that if you ask the world for great gifts, with absolute clarity, then you dramatically increase the chances of them happening. BUT you need to let go of being a control freak and trust that SPIRIT KNOWS THE FASTEST WAY!

grace

The two hardest tests on the spiritual road:
the patience to wait for the right moment
and the courage not to be disappointed
with what you encounter
—PAULO COELHO, *Veronika Decides to Die*

there is no doubt that accepting bad things
that come your way is an incredibly hard and challenging
thing to do. It's easy to find yourself in a position where you
begin to fight the world, but where does that get you? Angry
and frustrated is about it . . .

If you can be content to be exactly where you are and
embrace the lessons that come to you, then you give yourself an opportunity to grow through expansion. If you choose

instead to hold on to a fixed view of the world or of yourself, then you may find yourself getting upset or even depressed.

Why me? you may ask. *What did I do to deserve this?*

Muhammad Ali is someone who has had many highs and lows in his life. Most recently he has suffered from Parkinson's disease, which has rendered him, once known as the "Louisville Lip," almost mute. One could forgive Ali for being angry at the world for his current condition, but in 1989 Davis Miller interviewed him and asked about it:

> Miller: Does it bother you that you are a great man not being allowed to be great?
>
> Ali: You don't question God. I know why this has happened. God is showing me, and showing you [Ali points his shaking finger at Davis] that I'm just a man, just like everybody else.

If you're a fan of Ali, I'm sure you're not surprised by his dignified response, but what has amazed me is that he hasn't sought to hide himself from the world. Instead he has faced the world with an incredible amount of courage and dignity—lighting the Olympic flame for the 1996 Atlanta games with a shaking hand probably inspired as many people as his most valiant efforts in the ring. This once proud and some would say incredibly arrogant man has transformed himself into a humble and dignified statesman.

But how can you and I achieve such dignity and gracefully accept far less challenging circumstances than Ali? It's not an easy task, but again what choice have you got? You can fight the world, but all you will create is great angst within yourself.

If you can find faith that there is meaning to events and accept that as they occur you may not understand what the meaning is, then you are halfway there.

One way of doing this is to incorporate it into your daily meditation. You are what you believe, remember? Your story about yourself is all-powerful, so you need to put effort into changing your story.

In the mornings, take time to first still your mind—I outlined a way of doing this in *BE*. Once you have done this, consider how you are being in the world. Do you see yourself as being in complete control? If so, you need to let it go—don't give up on trying; that's not the idea here—rather simply submit your will to divine will. Set your intention not to fight the world but rather to accept things as they occur and be present to them.

You can waste a lot of energy complaining about the way things are, or you can choose to gracefully accept them. The choice is yours, but it will be much easier if you can find faith in the fact that life truly does have meaning.

remember to breathe

breathing along with the beating of your heart is one of the unconscious acts of the human body, but it's amazing how, when faced with challenging circumstances, we can sometimes forget how to breathe!

You may have taken the time in your morning meditation to set your intention not to fight the world when things don't go your way, but then you get to work, something happens, and the wheels begin to fall off.

BREATHE!

There are many different techniques you can use. Here's one adapted from an American Indian technique called the fourfold breath:

- Slowly breathe in through your nose, counting to four as you do so. Feel the oxygen circulate through your body, and imagine cleansing white light energy filling you up.

- Hold for a count of four, and continue to visualize the pure white light energy cleansing your system.

- Exhale through your mouth, counting to four as you do so. Feel the toxins being released from your system, and imagine any dark or negative energies flowing out of your body via the breath.

- Hold for a count of four, and feel your energy settling like the silt in a glass of dirty water.

- Repeat the process, each time feeling yourself getting lighter and more negativity leaving you.

It's a simple technique that you can do any time you feel negative emotions begin to overwhelm you or even if you are just tired. The technique oxygenates the body and activates the lymphatic system, which in turn helps to purge the toxins from your system.

Remember that the reason for doing all of this is so that you can be calm, focused, and—hopefully—nonreactive. As soon as you begin reacting to a situation you are out of control. Not only that, but as soon as you react, you are giving away your personal power and hence relinquishing your ability to have a say in the world that we are all continuously creating!

faith in one's self

forgive yourself

Notice the difference between what happens
when a man says to himself,
"I have failed three times,"
and what happens when he says, "I am a failure."
—S. I. HAYAKAWA

we all make mistakes—it's a simple fact of life. We all do things from time to time that we are not proud of. I talked about letting yourself off the hook in *BE* and *DO*, but there is a faith aspect to this as well.

Jason was a nice guy who had one major failing: when he was stressed he used to lose his temper easily and in frustration would yell at his girlfriend. When it happened the first time, he apologized profusely once he had calmed down, and resolved never to do it again. But a couple of weeks later, after a hard day at work he got into a petty argument about putting out the trash and started yelling again.

The next morning he'd calmed down, and once again he apologized and resolved not to lose control again. But one month later, just as he felt that he'd gotten on top of it, after a sleepless night due to a sick child, he found himself yelling at his girlfriend again.

Again, after calming himself down he apologized and said that he wouldn't do it again. But this time he started to doubt himself. He started to wonder if indeed he was simply an angry, out-of-control young man. His faith in himself and his ability to get over this issue began to waver.

The next time it happened, he gave up on himself. He resigned himself to the fact that he couldn't control his temper. He blamed his girlfriend for his outbursts and slowly he drove her away. From then on his story about himself was a very negative one, and he continued to create situations where he simply lost his temper until it became not only a judgment, but a habit.

Having faith in yourself means having faith that no matter what personal failings you see in yourself, you believe you can overcome them. We mustn't be afraid of our dark side.

If we start to believe negative judgments about ourselves, we effectively lock ourselves in a little box that quickly becomes very hard to get out of. If we argue for our limitations then—YES—we get to keep them.

Are you telling a story about yourself that you are not good enough or that you are a failure in some way? We are all on a journey! Few of us can say that we are just the way we want to be right now. Many of us are faced with situations where we love someone—whether it be a partner, parent, friend, or child—but they bring up a side of us that we simply don't like. Many of us are our harshest critics—and this can be especially so if you are trying to pursue a spiritual path.

Once again, we need to change the story. Remember that we are all created with divine potential; we can all do amazing things; we are all God's children.

If we buy into harsh judgments of ourselves, then not only do we deny ourselves the opportunity to work on these things, we also cop out on our responsibility. We give ourselves an excuse for why we are doing these things, and in turn we send ourselves down a road that becomes harder and harder to turn back from.

Gloria got married when she was very young. Not long after she got married, her boyfriend got in with a bad crowd and started habitually smoking marijuana. Gloria had never liked the stuff, but she really wanted to fit in, so she started smoking as well. Before long she found that she really needed to have a smoke at the end of the day.

When she visited her parents on her own for Christmas she tried not to smoke, but after a few drinks she found that she really, really needed a smoke, so she snuck outside to have a quick joint. Relieved but now stoned, she crept back to the Christmas party, only to be confronted by her fourteen-year-old niece, who peered oddly at her and then laughed.

Gloria freaked out. *How could I be such a bad person?* she wondered.

When she returned home, she didn't tell her husband what had happened, but the thought of it haunted her. He noticed the change in her. She seemed different, less self-confident. When he asked her about simple things like whether or not she had paid the bills, her responses were angry, and the resulting fights always seemed to end up with her accusing him of thinking she wasn't good enough for him. Slowly, she drove him away, which just served to reinforce to her that she indeed was not good enough.

Gloria tried to remain single, but another boyfriend came along. Self-doubts plagued her, and although she tried to hide it from him, their arguments began to end in the same way. "You don't think I'm good enough for you!" she would scream.

He was perplexed. He loved her, but he couldn't under-stand why she kept saying these things. Try as she might, her story about herself and the judgment she had came to rule her life.

We must forgive ourselves for our failings, but we must also have the courage to face up to them. Only by shining a light into the darkest corners of our personalities do we give ourselves the opportunity to heal. But we cannot be afraid of ourselves. We cannot try to push our dark side into a little bottle, push the stopper down, and then hide it away at the back of a cupboard. The interconnected nature of all of us means that on some level we feel it when someone is hiding something.

Face your harshest judgments about yourself. Have faith that anything can be solved if you have the will and the courage to DO SOMETHING ABOUT IT.

Hiding from the world doesn't serve you or us. Your pain is our pain, remember? Your happiness is our happiness. If one person is down, then we are ALL down.

get yourself out of the way!

Out beyond ideas of wrong doing and right doing
there is a field; I'll meet you there
When the soul lies down in that grass,
the world is too full to talk about
Ideas, language, even the phrase "each other"
doesn't make any sense.
—RUMI

if there is one universal truth—that we are all one—then an overwhelming focus on the "self" can only inhibit us from accepting the true nature of reality and ascending on a spiritual path.

But what is the "self" anyway, and what does it mean to "get yourself out of the way"?

I challenge you to find your "self." Is it your physical body, your mind, your emotions, your spirit? Or is it simply an intellectual construct that you have built up over time?

I believe that the "self" is simply a story we have built up over a long period of time based on the experiences we have had and the things that have been told to us. If we hold on to this "self," then by definition we hold ourselves separate from the world. We see our "self" and then we see the world through the eyes of that "self." The "self" then becomes a filter through which we put all experiences so that we can intellectually make sense of them.

But what is the nature of reality? Are we simply physical beings trying to be spiritual, or are we spiritual beings trapped in this physical realm? I believe we are the latter. I believe that in this realm we are the bridge between heaven and earth. The spiritual energy, or what the Chinese call *chi*, flows down from heaven into the top of our heads, through our bodies, and out into the earth.

I think the best analogy I have come across is that we are like bumper cars. We have a little thing that sticks up and makes contact with the energy, but if the energy isn't earthed then we go nowhere.

Many teachings propose that physical ailments are due to an energy blockage in the body. If we try to hold on to this energetic flow, then that is what we cause—a blockage. The trick is to let it go and not grasp the energy as it passes through us.

If we hold on to the "self," then by definition we are holding on to the story that we have constructed of who we are. As we feel energetic flows, instead of simply accepting them and honoring them, we try to interpret them with our mind. But if you do this it means that you are trying to clutch something and interpret it according to how you believe it should be . . . Hence you block yourself from seeing the true nature of reality and you block yourself from being able to grow. The stronger you try to hold on to your notion of self, the less able you will be to accept the natural flow of the Universe—the less able you will be to accept spirit and the growth that it brings you.

I know this is a hard thing to grasp, but are you trying to understand it with your mind or with your heart?

In *BE* I talked about how American Indians believe that we in the West relate to the world incorrectly, which in turn causes us unhappiness. They say that we try to receive with the mind, determine with the spirit, hold with the emotions, and then give with the body. In other words, we sit in our heads trying to work things out, then we try to decide what our gut feeling is about the various options. We hold our emotions back for fear of being hurt, then we give physical gifts to show our love for people. Instead, they say, we should receive with the spirit, determine with the mind, hold with the body, and give with the emotions.

If we are all one, then surely this makes a lot more sense, right?

Miranda was a corporate trainer. Before every new training session she would find that she became very nervous. She was very concerned about what people would think of her and whether or not they would give a good report back to their bosses at the end of the day.

At the beginning of every training session she would be very stiff and self-conscious. Her stiffness made the people in the training session even more aware of how she was being, so many would become quite judgmental of how she was acting. They would watch her movements even more closely than normal and pick up on any errors she might make.

But then there was always one bit of the training program that Miranda believed in deeply and was incredibly passionate about. When she would get to that particular part, suddenly her whole demeanor would change. Instead of thinking about her self-image and how she was being perceived, she would be focused on making sure the participants actually got the message.

The participants would feel the difference. They knew immediately that Miranda was now completely present to them instead of thinking about her "self," and she in turn was suddenly being much more powerful.

If we remain focused on the "self," then we deny ourselves the opportunity to be as powerful as we can truly be. We deny ourselves the opportunity to let the *chi* flow through us. We deny the ultimate truth about reality.

If we look at it from the perspective of the morphic field, we can get some idea of what happens from a scientific perspective. The morphic field links us all together.

Energies flow back and forth between us and all around us all of the time. If we are focused on the "self," then we grab the energies that we want and we reject energies that we don't want. We try to decide from our fixed point of view what suits us and what doesn't. We think that we are smart enough to work this out using our mind and our particular view of what fits and what doesn't. But all we end up doing is blocking the flow and preventing ourselves from truly experiencing reality as it is—rather than how we think it is.

If you worry that you won't get what you want unless you hold on tight and push, push, push to get it, what actually happens is that you get just the opposite because you give people such a hard time that you push them away.

Forget about the "self" for a moment, and let go of the fear that you won't be heard or that people won't care about you. Be present to them and give instead, trust in the universal law of karma, and an amazing thing will happen— you will get more than you could have possibly asked for or believed you deserved in the first place.

What does all of this have to do with faith?

Well, why do you want to hold on to and protect your notion of your "self"?

Are you afraid, like Miranda, that if you don't hold on to it then others will perceive you poorly?

Are you afraid that if you don't work on your "self"—from an intellectual or "head space"—then nothing will happen?

What makes you so sure that if you stop "trying" to make things happen from your "head space," they won't just happen naturally?

What makes you so sure that YOU know the best way to allow your spirit to grow?

If you only do what you think is right according to what you have rationally worked out using your mind, then you will only get what your limited knowledge and perception of the Universe can deliver to you. Your obsession with trying to receive with the mind blocks your ability to see the whole. You are in your own way . . .

How to get out of the way, then?

Let go of the "self," of course.

It's only a story, remember? To get over the story you need to have faith that you are a being of infinite potential and that you don't need to hold on so tight. You CAN let go.

In your morning meditations, once you have stilled your mind, "feel" where your energetic body is—it will most likely feel like a cocoon around you. Allow your sphere of energy to expand outward until it takes up the whole of the earth. (This is similar to the exercise that I outlined in *DO*, but the intention is different.) Don't see yourself as being separate from the earth and the other beings on it—see yourself as being at one with all things. Start the mantra, "There is no I, there is no me, there is no my . . ." As you say it in your mind, allow your "self" to begin to dissolve. Sit with this feeling for a while until you are ready to come back, and then allow yourself to return to your normal energetic sphere.

Before finishing, set your intention to be more aware of the interconnected nature of us all. When you become aware of energetic exchanges, don't try to grasp them, simply observe them and let them pass. When you feel yourself clutching a fixed idea of who you are, let it go. By doing this you will become more able to see yourself as part of the whole and to freely give without being in your own way.

courage

letting go of some of your fixed views of the world takes courage. Especially when many of the things that you need to believe in have little or no proof. When I meet people, I always try to find out what their view of the world is and how they actually live their life according to that view.

One such person was a rabbi who was working in Israel with people who on a daily basis were facing great challenges to their faith. He'd come to Australia to give some teachings, and I was lucky enough to spend some time with him.

As we were walking along I asked him what he prayed for. He explained to me that in the Jewish faith he believed that it was not possible to comprehend the hand of God in action. He said that with all of the bad things happening in the world, if one did this, it would be easy to deduce that God was somehow neglecting people, or even worse—that he was at times cruel.

Instead, he said, he prayed for the courage to simply and openly accept the challenges that were placed before him every day and to have faith that even though he might not understand the reasons behind God's actions, there was in fact a reason.

When you are faced with tests of your faith, this is a good thing to remember. Set your intention and make a request for things to be a certain way, but then let go of it. Pray for courage to have the strength to face whatever events come your way, and have faith that there is indeed a reason behind them.

what's your default position?

Some people spend a lifetime making good situations bad.
Others make bad situations good.
People who have a positive disposition are the
luckiest people, because they create their own luck!
It doesn't matter what happens to you,
it's how you deal with it that counts!
If the wheels fall off, then put them back on!
—ANONYMOUS

when nothing seems to be happening in your life and you sit down in your quiet space, what is the default position of your mind? Are you positive and peaceful about things or wracked with anxiety?

Over the years I've found many people who default into despair. But if you think about the world from the morphic field perspective, where does this leave you? Are you saying that you need a continual flow of evidence to make you happy and positive? Just because you're not getting it doesn't mean you are an unworthy or bad person.

The world never forgets about any of us, but if we default into despair, then we increase the chances of attracting experiences that reinforce that position. It's another one of those deadly loops, isn't it? And of course, it's another test of faith.

I love to write, but over the years I've also had to do various types of teaching and consulting work to pay my way. At times I've gone through periods where I've simply had no work. In those times I've often found myself despairing about how I was going to pay the bills that were due and whether or not some debt collector was going to come and repossess my things. When I'm in that mood, I can't write. My worries consume me.

But as soon as I start to snap myself out of it and decide to take the opportunity to write, I get a whole lot of work and I have no time to write.

Deadly, eh?

Looking back on those times, I can see that each one of them was a fantastic opportunity that I missed. Instead of being positive and having faith that things would come out right, I indulged myself in self-pity.

If you want to change your default position, then you need to do some more work to change your story. You can put as much energy into the expectation of good things as you can the expectation of bad things. It's totally up to YOU!

Once again, it's a meditation issue. If you fail to control your mind, you can be sure that you will fail to control anything else! If you have a negative story going on, then spend as much time as you can trying to still your mind. Once you have stilled your mind, start telling yourself a different story. There is meaning in life, and even though you can't understand what it is, you need to have faith that it will be revealed to you in time.

Stick some positive affirmations up on your wall if you find you have trouble changing your story.

NEVER WAIT, JUST DO!

We make our own luck, remember?

die a psychic death

One must have chaos within
to give birth to a dancing star
—FRIEDRICH NIETZSCHE

the end is nigh! Death of the old? Give into it completely with no fight—let go and embrace the new.

But what if you don't like the new?

Andrew was a good-looking guy who never had any trouble finding a girlfriend and had a great reputation for being a party animal. The problem was that as Andrew got older he really wanted to settle down and have some kids. He met a great girl, but he still wanted to party hard with his friends. He kept saying that he wanted to be more settled, stop partying, and be a father, but part of him kept fighting for his old life. He feared that letting go of the old would lead to a boring new life, just like all of the people he knew whom he had taken great delight in making fun of when they had to stay home and babysit while he went out and had fun.

Near the end of the journey, with the finish line in sight, you may stagger in a most distressing way—just as the biggest break you have ever had comes your way (like the woman or man of your dreams, the home you have always wanted, etc). Instead of bursting onward and upward, you are instead thrown to the ground and find you have to go back through every lesson you have learned along the way!

You will fight with indignation. *Why me? Why do I have to go through all of this again?* You may have all of the lessons you thought you had learned thrown at you at the same time or in quick succession of each other.

Let each old part of you die! Stop fighting and allow yourself to simply go with the flow!

You must go back step-by-step and check the story. Have you been telling yourself the right one? You must have FAITH that this is so before you can move on! Faith is the key! Faith that you have been on the right track and have not simply deluded yourself into believing that it is so.

Is your life path built on a stack of cards, or is it on a solid foundation of tested beliefs? You must check and be sure, because the energy required for the next step is so big that no energy can be wasted in constantly questioning the validity of the story thus far.

You must be strong and fully present—if part of you is still lingering in the past, then your energy will be there and doubts and fears will creep in.

Dying a psychic death will be VERY painful if you fight it! But how do you resist the urge to fight when a big part of you wriggles and squirms with the viciousness and desperation of a cornered tiger?

No, I don't want to let go of the image that I have of myself! you may say. *I want people to tell me how wonderful I am and how great I am, not question me and point out my bad side—press my emotional buttons to such an extent that I react in an angry and negative way!*

> [It isn't escapism] if you don't ever plan to come back . . .
> Wherever you are is reality.
> —DANIEL JOHNS, *lead singer of Silverchair*

You may think that at this point in the journey you are over that—that you have sorted out all of your "shit" and that you can embrace ALL people—no matter how offensive—with loving kindness and compassion. You may be in for a shock when confronted by a person who you cannot help but react to—you are faced instead with a mirror showing you your darkest side!

You may revile in horror. Struggle and turn to run. But alas, there is nowhere to go! You cannot run from the image you see before you, and not only that—you will not be able to forget what you have seen.

Try as you might to revert to your old self-image, the feeling will linger. This is when doubts creep in and begin to course through your body like a virus. *Am I really such a bad person?* you may ask yourself.

Faith . . . Faith in yourself! Your dark side will lure and tempt you—it is the easy path—*Come down this road,* it may say, *give up on these weird notions that you are good and somehow holy. All of that self-development stuff and spirituality talk is nonsense! The world of riches is right before you. Embrace your fear of others and honor your greed!*

Again, you may revile in horror.

But again you cannot run. Instead you must shine some light into these areas. Get down on your hands and knees in the sewer of your mind and start poking about. Why are you thinking these things? Why are you reacting in such a way? What deep-seated fear have you been hiding for so long that you don't even know what it is?

"A tiger named is a tiger tamed," goes the saying. You must find the tiger in your mind and name it. Only then can you begin to be free from it.

Maybe sometimes it is easier to have faith in others than it is to have faith in ourselves. But if we have faith in human nature as being fundamentally good, then we need to have faith not only in other's nature, but in our own!

A conscious recognition of this fact is required. Even when the demons within you speak, you must remember that we are not all pure, loving energy—we are light and

dark—our shadow side is there as our teacher to show us where we most need to shine some gentle, compassionate, loving energy.

Gentleness is the key. We must not beat ourselves up. We must not buy into and harness our own energy against ourselves. Forgiveness, gentleness, and compassion are vital. Without love for ourselves we are nothing. So PLEASE give yourself a break. Embrace love and bring it into your own life and the lives of others.

Standing at the abyss, all is not lost unless we BELIEVE it is!

> Thoughts that lie too deep for tears.
> —WILLIAM WORDSWORTH

what do you truly
believe you deserve?

For where your treasure is, there will your heart be also.
—MATTHEW 6:21

I guess you might have figured out by now that if we are all interlinked and YOU are a powerful being with the ability to cocreate the world, then it is vitally important to know EXACTLY what it is that you are putting out there.

If you don't BELIEVE that you deserve anything better than what you are getting, then YES, that is exactly what you will continue to get.

Take some time out now to think about a very good friend of yours. It should be someone whom you admire and hold dear in your heart. Imagine that this person has lost faith in themselves and is feeling very down about the world and their prospects for the future.

Take yourself off to somewhere quiet and think deeply about it for a moment.

Go on! Don't sit here and continue reading!

Now, write your friend a letter. Tell them how you really feel about them. What's special about them? What do you believe they deserve in life? Why?

Now, try and step outside of yourself. Imagine that you are a good friend of yourself. Imagine that you are in the same position as your friend—feeling down about yourself.

Take yourself off to somewhere quiet and think about what you would say to yourself. Now, write yourself a letter.

Read the letter back—is this the same as the story you tell yourself in your quiet moments?

If not, why not?

What makes you so sure that it is incredibly audacious to ask for such outrageous gifts from the Universe? Why are you so able to tell your friend that they deserve such things, but you cannot tell yourself?

Have faith . . . Not only in others, but in yourself!

Take the letter that you wrote to yourself and stick it up on a wall somewhere. Read it regularly until the story you tell yourself is the same as the letter.

DON'T WAIT FOR EVIDENCE before you start manifesting abundance in your life. The chicken lays the egg, not the other way around.

kill self-pity!

> Why get upset about something if it can be remedied?
> And what is the use of being upset about something
> if it cannot be remedied
> —Shantideva, *Tibetan Bodhisattva*

why is it so easy to gleefully accept the good things that come our way and take some responsibility for their manifestation, but so difficult to accept the bad things?

If you find yourself indulging in self-pity during such times, then you are denying two fundamental things that you must have faith in: first, that there is meaning in life, and second, that you are a cocreator in the Universe.

I hate to tell you this—and you probably don't want to hear it—but on some level you played a role in creating what you're getting now. Yes, I know this is rather harsh—

especially when it comes to tragic things such as terminal illnesses. But note that I said "cocreator," not "sole creator." This is where faith that there is meaning in life comes into the picture. And NO, I can't tell you what the meaning is behind why some people get sick and others don't. I could guess and suggest that it is something to do with learning specific lessons, but I don't know and I don't pretend to.

The point here is to look at situations where you are taking no responsibility and simply complaining about your lot in life. Why bother complaining? If it is something you can do something about—then DO IT! If it is something you can't do anything about, then WHY WASTE YOUR ENERGY?

If all you do is complain about things but take no action, then two things are happening—one, you are giving up your personal power and deferring to someone else, and two, you are being a pain in the ass!

Please don't waste your energy complaining. There are many other much more useful things you can do with it that honor yourself as a powerful and divine being.

While we are on this point, I should also point out the futility in comparison. There is NO comfort in comparison. If you are feeling down, there may be some very short-term relief from visiting someone who is feeling worse, but it will give you no long-term comfort. If you are feeling like someone is giving you a hard time, there is no point in giving them a hard time back and complaining about them or what they are doing.

Why? Because we are all interlinked, remember? My pain is your pain. It is not a zero-sum game. In other words, if you put someone else down to make yourself feel better, you are simply creating a situation that will eventually make you feel worse. You may be able to run from their wrath, but you will not be able to run from your conscience. If you complain about someone and justify it by saying that they complain about you, then all you will create is a situation where you are EXPECTING someone to complain about you, so you end up feeling that you must fire the first shot.

At some point you will look in a mirror and see what you have become. Then what are you going to do? Buy into the same game again? In the long run it will simply get you nowhere, because you are denying an essential truth—that we are all interlinked.

If you have faith that we are all interlinked, you will see that if you want to feel better about yourself, you should make someone else feel better. If you want people to stop complaining about you, stop complaining about them and lavishly dish out compliments instead. Try it—it works!

the 100 percent solution

Those who restrain desire do so because
theirs is weak enough to be restrained.
—William Blake

julie had finally found herself with a great man with whom she had fallen deeply in love, but she still felt that there were parts of herself that she needed to work on. Afraid that he would reject her if she revealed all of herself to her new man, she held back.

I think you might be able to guess what happens in this story.

If we have faith that we are truly interlinked and one, there can be no way of holding back without being detected on some level. A 90 percent solution produces a 90 percent result.

Remember the analogy I used of the bumper cars? Unless we are 100 percent present, we are holding on to something and blocking the energy that flows through us. We are not only denying ourselves the opportunity to be 100 percent of who we really are, we are also denying the Universe to give us a 100 percent result.

Holding back means you only hold yourself back from receiving 100 percent in return. It may seem like a good idea at the time—many things do. You may be able to justify it by saying you are scared or fearful of what might happen if you reveal 100 percent of yourself. But one of the greatest gifts we can give to one another is 100 percent of ourselves—in wholeness and completeness.

Let's go back to Julie for a moment. She's afraid that her boyfriend will reject her if she tells him about the fears that she has or some of the failings she has had in her life. Richard, the boyfriend, sees it completely differently. He feels that on some level she IS holding something back. He asks her about it, but of course she denies it and says everything is fine.

Richard starts to wonder what is going on. As is the way of the human mind, he begins to make up stories in his head—that Julie doesn't really love him, Julie is having an affair, Julie doesn't really need him, and so on.

His suspicions drive him to push her further, and as he pushes her, she gets more protective of those little skeletons in her closet. She becomes more and more fearful of telling him the REAL 100 percent truth about herself. The more she tries to protect herself—all with what she sees is good intent—the more he feels that she is not being present to him.

Eventually, they have a big argument. He demands to know what's going on. She really wants to tell him—she's told her friends and her mother already—but her fear stops her from telling him.

Are you living your life 100 percent? Warts and all? Are you embracing life and honoring the sacred flow of events, or are you trying to control things again?

If not—what are you waiting for?

Look at it this way—what have you got to lose? If your relationship fails because you can't tell someone how you really feel, is it better than it failing because you've told them all about yourself and they've decided you're the wrong person for them? If you're making a presentation to a packed auditorium, is it better to be self-conscious and boring than to stumble and fall off the stage while passionately trying to make a point? I think not.

As with many things, young children provide us with shining examples of how to live 100 percent. How many young children fall into bed at night utterly exhausted from the day's events? They are tired because they don't hold back. They don't bother to protect themselves, because they don't know that they should—nobody has bothered to teach them that yet.

FAITH

Being 100 percent there means that you have to have faith in others, faith in yourself, and faith in the fact that life has meaning. If you find that you are holding back, consider this for a moment and think about what sort of energy you are putting out there into the morphic field. What are you inviting to come back to you?

Again, what have you got to lose?

If you are going to fail, you may as well fail greatly! Give 100 percent and embrace the results. You will certainly find that things will start to move along at a much more rapid pace, and you'll end up getting to where you are headed much more quickly!

fear

Fear, even the smallest fear,
is a hacking at the chords of faith.
—ANONYMOUS

ah! Now we are getting to the nitty-gritty, aren't we?

Fear the deadly demon of the mind!

I love those workshops you can go to where they say, "Feel the fear and do it anyway!" "Yay! Let's do it!" we all scream as we run from the auditorium completely pumped up by an inspirational speaker and ready to take on the world.

But then reality bites, doesn't it? You get back home, sit down to write the poem you've been planning for years, pick up the phone to tell your boss to go shove it, or start typing a text message to dump your boyfriend—then the "what ifs" begin.

Fear stops us from embracing our freedom and taking on our full power, because it blocks us up. I talked about this in *BE* and *DO*, but again let's look at it from the context of faith. If you have faith that there is meaning in life, then fear of future events becomes irrelevant. Fear will simply stop you from being 100 percent present, which, as we discussed earlier, means you get a less than 100 percent solution. If you can find faith in yourself as a divine being, then fear of failure also takes on less power.

Overcoming fears requires self-discipline. I discussed a method for achieving this in *DO*, but faith in yourself, faith that there is meaning in life, and faith in others will give you the strength to face what you are afraid of.

Buddhism teaches that there are four essential truths: that life is suffering, that there is a cause to suffering, that there is an end to suffering, and that there is freedom from suffering.

Our fears dictate to us because we let them! Once a fear arises, it triggers an emotion in us and we begin to tell ourselves a story. Our stories are all-powerful, remember? So if the story we are telling ourselves is a negative one, then yes, we create it! We put that energy out there into the morphic field, and not only do other people feel it on some level, but they also react to it.

So meditation once again becomes important. Sit quietly and still your mind. Allow your fears to arise. Visualize them and face them. Don't have aversion to them. That will only serve to give them more energy. Focus on your breathing as you feel the fear begin to tighten your stomach and restrict your abdomen. BREATHE . . . Let the power that the fear has over you leave your body as you exhale. Every time you find your mind beginning to tell yourself a story in reaction to the fear—stop it. Go back to your breathing. Tell yourself another story instead. Tell yourself about how you are a divine and powerful being. Tell yourself you have faith that life has meaning. Tell yourself that you will no longer be ruled by your fears. Tell yourself that you are now going to live life 100 percent and accept whatever comes your way regardless of what it is.

Overcoming our fears requires work, but we also need to have faith. Faith will give you the ability to believe in something that has no proof, and in turn it will help you to create something seemingly impossible. Without faith we cannot believe, and without belief we cannot create.

everything repeats

have I said this already? Just kidding . . .

But yes, everything repeats. Before you can move along to the next lesson or stage in your life, you will find that everything you have already learned along the way will come back to you to check and see if you have it figured out.

Reject these experiences as much as you like, but if you do you won't be going any further along the journey.

Instead, if you realize that you are going through a repeated lesson, accept that either you didn't get it the first time, you still need to learn something else, or that the Universe is just checking.

Either way, you should recognize, if you can find the space and peace of mind not to throw your toys out of the crib, that it is an exciting sign that you are ready to move on . . .

FAITH

The next few chapters focus more specifically on how you can maintain faith in other people and the notion of oneness—especially when confronted with some, shall we say, more challenging characters.

faith in others and the nature of oneness

your picture is not the
whole picture

Each lifetime is the pieces of a jigsaw puzzle. For some
there are more pieces. For others the puzzle is more
difficult to assemble. But know this: you do not have within
yourself all the pieces of your puzzle. Everyone carries within them at least one and probably many pieces to someone
else's puzzle... When you present your piece,
which is worthless to you, to another, whether you
know it or not, whether they know it or not, you are
a messenger from Most High.
—Rabbi Lawrence Kushner

I used the quote above in *DO* and I hope you will forgive
me for repeating it here, as I think it is a profound piece of
wisdom.

As you go along the road of life and begin to BE who
you want to BE and DO what you want to DO, you will most

likely begin to believe that you have things figured out. After delving deeply into your "self" you will feel that you have some degree of understanding of the nature of reality. You may begin to believe that your view of the world is a pretty close approximation for how things actually are.

WRONG AGAIN . . .

Imagine that the true nature of reality is a three-dimensional holographic sphere (I think it would be more correct to say it's four-dimensional, but let's not get into that now). Each one of us is also a much smaller three-dimensional holographic sphere, and we are all inside the big sphere. Some of us are at the top of the sphere, some to one side, some at the bottom. Pulsating through the sphere and through all of us is energy.

Are you with me so far? Go and get a globe or a big ball if it's easier, and imagine that we are all little balls within the big ball.

Now, from our position within the sphere we are able to perceive different parts of the sphere, and this forms our perception of reality. From our limited viewpoint, we may initially only be able to see out through one side of our own sphere, but as we do "work" on ourselves, we slowly but surely polish off the muck from all over our sphere that stops us from seeing out in every direction.

When we have polished our sphere as much as we can, our rational minds tell us that we have dealt with all of our "shit" and become quite enlightened. If we look in any direction, we can see clearly, unencumbered by our own stories and baggage. We may even start to tell people how to clean the muck off their own spheres, or if we are really silly we might start writing books about the stuff.

But here's the trick—don't be fooled into believing that your interpretation of reality is the same as reality itself!

You may think that you can see everything there is to see, but guess what? Your sphere is rigidly fixed in one place, and you are simply seeing the world from one viewpoint.

Real enlightenment comes when you are able to not only see clearly through every aspect of your sphere, but to also move your sphere around the larger sphere so that you can truly adopt other views on the nature of reality.

Think about that for a second . . .

We say that it's good to be able to put ourselves in another person's shoes, but what does that really mean? Are you putting yourself in their shoes as you PERCEIVE them to be, or are you really dropping YOUR view of reality and adopting theirs?

It's a good question, isn't it?

So how could you adopt someone else's view of reality? Well, for one, accept that no matter how right you think you are—YOU MAY BE WRONG.

If you are asking people questions about what they think of the nature of reality but all of the time you are simply comparing it to your view of reality, then all you are doing is seeing if their view fits with your view. You are interpreting it from your viewpoint.

The only way is to truly listen and to feel on an intuitive level where they are coming from—in other words, receive with the spirit and stop trying to rationally work something out with just your mind.

Yes, this is incredibly hard to do, but it is most rewarding and enlightening, because it starts to open you up to new ways of looking at the world and begins to set you free of your fixed view of the world.

Of course, to do this requires faith in others and the ultimate nature of oneness. If you can begin to see others as a part of a greater whole that includes you, then begin to open the door and let them in.

Just remember, the next time someone really challenges your view of the world or pushes your buttons, they may in fact be trying to give you a gift of perception that you simply cannot get to all by yourself.

engage

We cannot expect to take part in the race
without disturbing the water,
or expect to win it without making waves.
—ANONYMOUS

there is a story about a man who went off to
the mountains of Tibet and sat in a cave for years in search
of enlightenment. For years and years he kept to himself,
meditated for many hours every day, and struggled with his
inner demons.

When he had found peace within himself, he left the
cave and headed off to—where do you imagine?

New York—to become a taxi driver . . .

Why? It's relatively easy to go off and be by yourself and

find a sense of spirit but never engage with others. But that just denies the truth that we are all one. It's much harder to dip a toe in the water and make some ripples.

By engaging with other people, we give ourselves the opportunity to see into a mirror—to see how our actions affect others and how they are in turn reflected back to us. Sometimes we don't like what we see, sometimes we are challenged by it, but there are always opportunities for growth. The point here is that in order to accept life's opportunities you need to have faith in the nature of oneness.

Note here also that there is a great benefit in taking one's self off to the mountains for some serious self-reflection. The nature of interconnectedness means that if some people are sitting in the mountains in a quest to find enlightenment, then all of us benefit from such actions.

People have tried this as well. There are instances where experienced meditators have gone into high crime areas and simply sat every day and meditated on loving kindness —and the crime rate went down.

Many prayer and meditation groups have been formed all around the world for various causes. If you have faith in the interconnected nature of all of us, then you will be able to see just how and why these types of actions work.

But I digress . . . The point is that one mustn't be afraid to engage with others and also to accept that, YES, you may

make some ripples along the way, but that is just part of the learning process.

> Beauty is eternity gazing at itself in a mirror.
> But you are eternity and you are the mirror.
> —KAHLIL GIBRAN

stop telling the story, stupid!

Ours is an age of distraction. The background to our lives
is a white noise of inconsequential television programs,
pompous pundits, shrill talk-back callers, ten-second news
grabs and the cult of celebrity.
In this environment the need for contemplation and some
introspection becomes compelling—a time to stop,
to think, to make our way, guided by a moral compass,
a bearing that devines by our best instincts. . . .
The way people think of themselves in the cosmos
will affect the way they behave in the physical framework
of their lives.

—PAUL KEATING, *former prime minister of Australia*

we've already discussed the power of our
story, but it is worth reiterating here. The media bombards
us on a daily basis with negative images and stories about

the bad things that humans do to each other. With such an overload of negative information, it is very easy to find yourself sitting and having your hair cut or chatting to a friend and recounting the horrible things that you have seen on the news or read in the paper.

If our story is so powerful and what we believe helps create the world, then WHY ARE YOU TELLING THE STORY?

I stayed at a friend's house for a while when America was considering invading Iraq in 2003. Not only was this friend very intelligent, but his house was also a great meeting place for a wider group of very intelligent and thoughtful people.

In that house the papers were delivered daily, the Internet connection was super-fast broadband, and the television was able to receive all sorts of news channels from all over the world. To say that we were bombarded with information would be an understatement.

Being intelligent and thoughtful people, we all started coming up with pet theories about what would or wouldn't happen in the future, and we all started selectively gathering evidence to support our particular view. The problem was that many of those views were very negative—including things like Saddam Hussein had nuclear weapons that he would fire at Israel and begin a third world war.

Before too long we'd started trying to work out how far a radioactive nuclear blast cloud would spread, whether or not we'd be affected, and what we would then do about it.

Useful? Not really . . .

If you find yourself repeatedly telling a story about how mankind is evil, then consider what you are assisting to create in the world.

If the story is being fed by a constant bombardment of negativity from the media, then STOP WATCHING THE NEWS OR READING THE PAPER!!!!!

I promise you that you will miss out on very little, and your peace of mind will be much better.

Oh, and if you just need the sports pages or the funnies, then have the discipline to read just those parts and STOP reading when you get to the negative bits.

The same goes for when you meet up with people who begin a conversation with, "Did you see on the news what happened to those people when . . . "

STOP! No, thank you . . . It's very simple. Negativity breeds negativity and it eats away at your faith in human nature. Turn it around—start looking for good news stories and telling them instead. I promise you there is always plenty to talk about.

we are all flawed

We are here to ruin ourselves and break our hearts
and love the wrong people and die.
—NICHOLAS CAGE'S CHARACTER IN *MOONSTRUCK*

do you know a perfect person—someone who never does anything wrong or never has a harsh word to say about another?

I doubt it. Part of the human condition is that we are all flawed. I remember reading an interview with the Dalai Lama in which he was asked whether or not he had bad sides to his character. In his own humble way he explained that, yes, sometimes he finds anger arising in his mind over the most trivial of things.

We need to recognize that all humans are flawed beings. We all make mistakes. When others make mistakes it is easy to get on their case, tell them exactly how and why they have made the mistake, and judge them harshly.

But where does that get us?

If we are to have faith in others, then we must accept this as a simple fact of life. Instead of judging people, what we need to do is acknowledge what has happened, forgive them, and then hold out a space for them for the highest possibility. Hold a higher space for love, truth, and future possibilities.

John was a successful corporate raider in the heady days of the late eighties. Over a decade or so he built up a huge empire of companies and made millions and millions of dollars. But in the process he gained a reputation for being ruthless and at times unethical.

With the harder times of the nineties, fortune turned against him. As the economy stopped growing, his asset base began to shrink, and as it did he found that his debts began to drag his empire down. Slowly but surely, he lost each little bit of it until in the end he found himself with just a small shell of a company.

The media, which had once lauded praise upon him, now took great delight in vilifying him. He got into serious legal trouble. His marriage fell apart. Once-faithful business allies took potshots at him, and loyal friends seemed to disappear.

But among the smoldering ruins of his empire, an amazing thing happened: he realized the error of his ways and changed his beliefs.

When questioned by the media, he tried to express his sorrow for what had happened and to explain his newfound view on life, but they would have none of it.

Judgment had locked him in a nasty little cage—there was no opportunity for him to be heard. No one held out any space for him to be a better man.

Remember that if we hold someone down, then some part of us must be down there with them. If we buy into a harsh judgment about them, then WE stop them from becoming who they might be, and in turn we deny ourselves the opportunity to benefit from their uplift.

Faith without unity is a one-legged man. You may be able to stand, but you will have difficulty walking. We need to have faith in the ability of others to see the error in their ways and grow. We need to hold out the highest possibility for others so at least there is a space that they can shift to. What I mean by that is we need to hold on to the possibility that others really can be everything we wish them to be. Without that we trap them and ourselves.

paranoia will destroy ya!

what do you do when people repeatedly screw you over?

Rachel was an interior designer whose passion was creating buildings that not only provided a great environment for people to work in but also were environmentally friendly. Frustrated in her current role, where she more often than not ended up renovating buildings for developers who had no interest in the environment, she began to look for a new job.

Soon after she began her search she found herself at an industry function sitting next to Brian, an affable middle-aged man who began telling her that he was setting up a new design consultancy. Hardly believing her luck, she discreetly mentioned that she might be interested in a new job. The only problem was that Brian knew the people who ran her current company very well. Nevertheless, he agreed

that he would try to work out a solution and said he would contact her in the near future.

Two weeks went by before Brian phoned. He told her he was now ready to employ her but asked that she avoid telling her employers where she was going and instead simply resign stating personal reasons.

Rachel did this and soon found herself in a new job feeling very positive about the prospects of working closely with Brian. However, Brian seemed to be preoccupied with getting the business off the ground and was rarely in the office. In his place she found Robert, a man who to her seemed extremely ambitious and intent on assuming the managerial role in the new company.

Rachel didn't like Robert. She found him to be shallow and a bit slippery. Although he was always pleasant to her, something deep inside of her told her not to trust him. One day when Brian came into the office, she found the time to corner him for a quick chat. Not wanting to rock the boat in her new company, she put her fears to one side and instead gently asked him what Robert's role was.

Brian avoided her question and instead gave her a long speech about how important it was to get out there and get some business. "Sales are the name of the game at the moment," he boldly announced.

Rachel's heart sank. Sales were her worst nightmare. She wanted to concentrate on design. But she could see that since the company was just starting out, she would have to get out there and find some business. So off she went to knock on doors and drum up business so that she could, she believed, get back into the office and concentrate on designing inspiring work environments.

Months passed by, and as they did Robert seemed to be taking more and more control over the company. Every time she tried to bring up her need and wish to get back to design, Robert told her that she would need to find more business, because there simply wasn't the budget for her to just concentrate on design. More than once he implied that she "owed" them something because they had headhunted her from a company run by associates of theirs.

Rachel's self-confidence wavered, but instead of confronting Brian on what he had promised her, she continued to keep her fears to herself. Paranoia began to overwhelm her thoughts and affect her behavior. At the weekly meetings she found herself vigorously defending her sales record rather than honestly admitting that it was not her passion. Every time she looked at Robert sitting pompously at the head of the boardroom table, new fears and paranoia arose in her.

Finally she began to think that they were actually trying to get rid of her, and at the end of her tether she lost control in a board meeting and resigned.

Rachel saw herself as the victim. THEY had promised many things and had not delivered. THEY had destroyed her self-confidence. THEY, THEY, THEY . . .

FAITH

But what role did Rachel play in all of this?

She had lost faith in herself and had given her power over to others. Instead of facing her fears, she had bought into her paranoia and it had eaten away at her.

WE ARE ONLY VICTIMS IF WE BELIEVE WE ARE.

Imagine if Rachel had instead resolved to have faith in other people and the interconnected nature of us all. If she was feeling negative about Robert, then surely both he and Brian would pick up on it on some level, and her role was simply to make them aware of this by being more explicit. Instead of fearing what *they* might do, she may instead have simply told them how *she* was feeling.

At the end of the day we cannot avoid the lessons that the Universe wishes to give us. If you are confronted by feelings of doubts about others, why not simply share those feelings? Don't be a victim; take responsibility for what you are creating in the world.

don't be afraid to ask the hard questions

I disapprove of what you say,
but I will defend to the end your right to say it.
—VOLTAIRE

tough or uncomfortable interactions with others are simply opportunities to learn more about ourselves.

But—yes, another big BUT—don't have blind faith in others. Don't dishonor your feelings and put them aside because you are paranoid or afraid. If you have doubts or fears about others, then TEST your faith. Take a deep breath and gently and compassionately take the time to ask people the hard questions.

If you are afraid to do this, ask yourself why. Are you afraid of the result? If your fears are correct, then what have you got to lose by bringing things to the surface now? Are you afraid of the reaction of the person you are asking?

Manfred was an emotionally unbalanced chef. He took great delight in ruling his kitchen through fear and regularly threatened people either directly or by implication. Even his boss, Julian, was afraid of him. When Julian wanted to ask Manfred about why the kitchen was dirty or why there was spoiled food in the fridge, he would try as much as he could to delegate the task to someone else. When Julian did find the courage to ask Manfred tough questions, Manfred often simply walked away as Julian was talking to him and would then go for days on end without speaking or even looking at Julian.

Even though Julian had his doubts about Manfred's ability in the kitchen and his lack of cleanliness, his fear stopped him from ever being able to truly question whether his faith was misplaced. The result was that instead of his mind being clear and settled, it was plagued with nagging doubts. Late at night he would lie awake wondering what to do, but he was paralyzed by fear—*What if? . . . What if? . . . What if? . . .*

But what about faith in the notion of interconnectedness?

If something or someone is troubling you, fearful inaction will not serve you or the other person. Manfred's actions had impact not only on Julian but on all of the other staff members who had to work with him. By saying and doing nothing Julian was by implication supporting Manfred's

behavior. Part of being proactive is having the ability to face your fears and confront uncomfortable situations.

Fear is fed by FEAR. There is nothing to fear but fear itself. Dark or negative energies draw their power from your dark side. You must allow light to shine into those areas. Have faith in the true power of light and love. Don't let fear rule you. Don't let others dictate to you through fear. Be brave enough to gently and compassionately ask the hard questions. Don't just have blind faith, as it will simply make you blind.

> Darkness cannot drive out darkness;
> only light can do that.
> Hate cannot drive out hate;
> only love can do that.
> —MARTIN LUTHER KING JR.

the truth will set you free

The man who fears no truths
has nothing to fear from lies.
—THOMAS JEFFERSON

i guess you may have already figured out that the key to living a life based on faith is the willingness to wholeheartedly—and fearlessly—embrace and speak the truth.

Speaking the truth is not just about being moral; it is about being truthful with yourself. Without honoring your own truth you will hinder your progress on a spiritual path, because you are dishonoring your connection with the sacred.

Close relationships are one of the hardest areas in which to speak the truth, especially if what you really feel

is something you believe may hurt the other person. At these times it seems easier to avoid telling the truth or to soften it in some way.

But where will that get you? If you don't tell the truth, you will be separating yourself from others by not being inclusive.

Remember the morphic field? We've already discussed what can happen in relationships when people "feel" that they are not getting the whole story.

The key is to be able to separate how you feel about a person's behavior from how you feel about them. This can only be done in an environment of inclusiveness and love.

We need to honor the fact that we come together in relationships to help each other learn. We do this by providing a mirror for each other. If we don't tell each other the truth, we aren't providing an accurate mirror. We are distorting the reflection, and by doing so we are denying the other person the opportunity to see the real effect they are having on others and the opportunity to grow and learn from the experience.

Communication is the trick here, and you can't just wait for it to happen. You need to be brave enough at some point to set your intent to have an honest and truthful relationship. Have faith that the other person truly loves you, and have faith that we are all interconnected. If you can be brave enough to set things up in your relationship so that you both know you are committed to each other and each other's growth, then you will begin to have the basis for speaking the truth without fear of the consequences.

Early in your relationship you need to give each other permission to gently and carefully point out behaviors that are out of line with your commitment to each other. If you don't trust your commitment to each other, it is very easy for the other person to see any truthful feelings that reflect negatively on their behavior as reflecting negatively on their character. We are not our behavior—that is only something that we have learned over a period of time. If our behavior is out of alignment with who we desire to be, then surely we need to know about it.

Who better than to provide an opportunity for personal growth than a good friend or companion?

Let me reiterate here. If you haven't had an honest conversation about making a commitment to supporting each other and gently and compassionately speaking the truth, then your truth may simply be interpreted as an attack on the other person's character.

Remember, keep it simple here. Make a commitment, be 100 percent present, speak the truth gently and compassionately, AND remain there to support the other person in whatever comes up for them.

If you've only been 70 percent truthful in your relationship so far, then you also need to remember that old habits die hard. Having faith in each other is much easier said than done. It can be very difficult not to react negatively when an aspect of your behavior is pointed out to you that you REAL-LY do not like. It's easy to turn around and point the finger back at the other person. It's much harder to take a deep breath, accept that the other person is there with you, and set your intention to work on it.

Only by having faith in others and the nature of oneness can we find the space to open our hearts and embrace the truth in the spirit of inclusiveness.

Oh, and one more thing. Don't spend hours and hours gathering the courage to tell the other person how you truthfully feel with an expectation of what the outcome will be. YOU MAY BE WRONG, remember? Your picture is not the whole picture.

Gentleness, compassion, and an open mind go hand in hand with speaking the truth.

words are not enough

There is no need to talk, because the truth of
what one says lies in what one does.
—BERNHARD SCHLINK

because of the interconnected nature
of us all, if one's actions don't reflect one's words, then on
some level we all know it. Don't kid yourself that this isn't
true or you will be in for a rude awakening!

You may truly and deeply love your kids, for instance, and
you may tell them this often, but all of us watch behavior.
If you never spend any time with them, don't be surprised
if they doubt the truth of your words in some way.

BE who you are.

If the message that we are getting from our hearts
doesn't match our heads, no amount of intellectual ration-

alizing will remove the uneasy feeling we have that something is WRONG . . .

Mary met a great guy named Gabriel. He was just the type of person she had been looking for—intelligent, financially secure, and on a spiritual path in life. Her head kept telling her how perfect he was for her, but she'd been hurt in the past so she protected her heart just a little bit—just in case he lost interest and unceremoniously dumped her.

Gabriel loved Mary with all of his heart despite the fact that she had her flaws. "We all have flaws," he would say when she lost her temper for no apparent reason and said nasty things to him. He stayed in that space with his heart wide open even when she did little things that hurt him. Mary sometimes worked on weekends, but she hated him going out without her, which she told him in no uncertain terms. He'd ask her if she would mind, to which her reply was often quite venomous. "I've been wanting to go out with you for a long time, and I'd be really hurt if you went out without me," she would say.

But from time to time Gabriel had work commitments at night, and Mary wouldn't hesitate to go out with the girls for a wild night of partying. When Gabriel tried to ask her about this, it always resulted in her pointing the finger at him and saying things like, "YOU always think of yourself. It's always ME, ME, ME with you, isn't it? Why can't you think of me for a change?"

Finally, after months of going around and around in the same familiar loop, Gabriel asked Mary if she really did love him and whether or not she really was committed to him. Immediately, she sprang up and gave him a long speech about why they were meant to be together and how "right" their relationship felt to her. In her head she was desperately trying to work out a way of getting herself out of the negative behavioral loop she found herself in. All she really had to do was open her heart and tell him how she felt, but out of habit she just kept trying to CONTROL the situation so that she wouldn't get hurt. But to Gabriel the words didn't ring true. Something inside of him told him that she wasn't really "there," that even though her head was committed, her heart was well and truly protected.

Have you been in a situation like Mary's? Did you try really hard to work out how to resolve it using your powers of reasoning? Did you try to CONTROL the situation? All along were you actually really SCARED? Did your stomach tie itself up in knots while you used all of your energy to protect yourself from getting hurt?

"The truth will set you free" really does mean THE TRUTH WILL SET YOU FREE! If you tell little lies (white lies, one might say) because you are scared of the truth, and if you think you can find a way to the end result that you desire without having to fully reveal yourself—you are just deluding yourself.

But it's not enough just to say the truth. You have to BE the truth. Not BEING truthful doesn't just hurt others; it denies you the opportunity to grow. By trying to control the situation, you also hinder the flow of energy through you and hence deny the flow of spirit. By trying to control others, you dishonor their freedom and in turn dishonor your own. Their freedom is your freedom.

The only way to truly honor people is to open your heart to them. This of course requires FAITH in others.

The flipside to this of course is that if you make a commitment to truly BE there for someone and they respond by freaking out and you begin to feel that it is all too much, you can't run away . . .

Oops, there goes that out . . .

Some relationships come to an end—that is the way of life. If two people come together for a specific reason—maybe to teach each other something—then sometimes when that exchange is finished they part ways. But running is a whole different story. It will feel different—there won't be that sense of completion. Instead of sadness about what has happened, you may instead feel anger.

But we can't run from life's lessons . . . If you have faith that life has meaning and that we are all interconnected, then you will know that all people come into our lives for a reason. If you run because you aren't brave enough to face the lesson, all that will happen is that you will get another teacher—maybe a harsher teacher.

If you have faith that life's lessons repeat until we face them, then you have nothing to fear from other people and you have nothing to fear from not only speaking but in LIVING the TRUTH.

All of those worries and fears that you have about yourself become less important if you can have faith. If you want someone to love you for who you are, then BE who you are—ALL of who you are! Not just the bits that you feel comfortable enough to show someone else.

I must point out to you here that this is not an incremental thing. It's not something you WORK on. It's called a LEAP OF FAITH because you have to LEAP—if you don't leap, by definition you fall into the abyss.

You don't go from being 70 percent there to 80 percent to 90 percent to 100 percent.

You make a leap from 70 percent to 100 percent, boots and all . . .

But once you make that leap, you may suddenly find that your fears grab hold of you again and make you jump back to the other side.

You must remember that everything repeats for a reason. Gather your courage and make the leap of faith again!

If you are with someone who tells you they love you but they are protecting their heart because they are scared, remember to BE GENTLE! These behaviors are OLD patterns that grab onto us tightly and don't let go without a BIG fight! If you react with anger and frustration, you will only serve to drive the other person away. This is NOT being who you say you are BEING. This is not being committed.

Compassion rises up when one knows the heartfelt truth—lies only give rise to anger and frustration. A truthful heart knows when it feels the truth, because it resonates deeply. Blame is a pointless exercise—the truth will set you free on both levels.

Whatever situation you are in and whatever side of the equation you are on, remember when your fears arise that you are not good enough or that you may get hurt—have faith, take a deep breath, and find the courage to speak your truth and BE it.

the spiral of
selflessness

People without hearts . . . have lost the capacity
to experience the deep generational bond to
other humans and to their surroundings . . .
Without my land and my people—
I am simply flesh waiting to die.
—JEANETTE ARMSTRONG, *Canadian Indian*

there is a spiral that leads to ascension. It is the path that frees you from the bounds of human suffering and takes you closer to your true being—or divine nature. It spirals upward and it also spirals downward.

The steps along the spiral are taken through selfless service. We get onto the path by having faith that we are all one. When we let go of the self and abandon fear and doubt, then the spiral of faith and trust in others goes upward. When we

have faith that if we let go then all will be okay, we are truly aligned to the fact that we are all one.

We go along this path until something happens to shake our faith in others. Then we withdraw. This is simply a test of faith, but withdrawing just sends us down the spiral. We start protecting ourselves and looking after our own interests first. We may SAY that we are there for others, but ALL of us is not there; some of us is holding back, looking after ourselves—just in case . . .

But as we buy into this view of the world, it sends us down the spiral until we get so desperate and deluded about the void of meaning in our lives that we find we must refocus and find our faith again. When we are desperate enough and nothing makes any sense anymore and we know that we can't understand the Universe by ourselves—with our minds alone—we turn to something else that may give us guidance. We ask for help from God or from the universal spirit.

When we do this we find that we must have faith again, and hence we start going back up the spiral.

The interesting thing about the spiral is that as we travel up and down, each time we fall down a little way we don't fall all the way back to where we were the last time. We ascend.

But we can only continue to ascend if we continue to have faith, and we can only continue to have faith if we have the courage to act on our faith and live it.

This is the absolute truth. It is simple! We are all one—individually we are NOTHING.

So what have you got to lose?

FAITH

PUTTING IT ALL TOGETHER

the path of virtue

When you find the way others will find you.
Passing by on the road they will be drawn to your door.
The way that cannot be heard will be echoed in your voice.
The way that cannot be seen will be reflected in your eyes.
—Lao-Tzu

there are a lot of words in this book, and I think it is easy to get caught up in the stories and miss the simplicity of the message. So for those of you who like sixty-second book summaries, I believe there is a series of questions you can ask yourself that will help to make sense of everything I have presented to you here. As you go through the questions and the steps involved, ask yourself what you truly believe and whether or not this belief has served you in living a good and happy life.

Are you challenged by the world?
Do you have faith that life has meaning?
(FAITH IN LIFE)

Do you believe that you have the capacity to face the challenges that come your way?
(FAITH IN ONE'S SELF)

Do you believe human nature is ultimately good or bad?
(FAITH IN OTHERS)

If good, then do you believe that we can create a better world?
(HOPE)

What stops us?
What prevents us from embracing our freedom and fulfilling our full potential?
(FEAR)

How do we overcome fear?
(SELF-DISCIPLINE)

What will be your guide?
Examples include:
Buddhism (equanimity—an end to suffering)
Christianity (make yourself an empty vessel and
fill yourself with the spirit of the Lord)
Other spiritual or warrior teachings (stop the world)

How do you accept the bad things that
may happen along the way?
How do you let go of the idea that you know best?
How do you seize the opportunity in the present and
seize your gift of power?
How do you stop fighting the world?
(GRACE)

How do you have a pure heart and put good into the world?
How do you feed your own soul?
What is your selfless service?
(CHARITY and COMPASSION)

How do you live the life that your soul has chosen for you?
Are you living it?
(COURAGE)

Embrace Life!
Be grateful for every moment and live it like it is your last!
(FREEDOM)

FAITH

In going down a spiritual life path you will see that ultimately we seek our own freedom. But what is freedom?

Once we are free from any sort of oppression by others, the ultimate freedom is freedom from the self. For the ultimate battle is the battle within the self.

Mastering our fears, doubts, and anxieties is surely the highest task that is given to us in this lifetime. For if we can master our own fears, we can then go forth into the world and help others to master theirs. This is the interconnected nature of reality and the task that confronts us all.

the mystical solution

"Any last words of wisdom you can give us?"
the student asked. The mystic thought for a moment.
"You can work out just about any difficulty you have by
remembering two sentences."
"What are they?"
"Number One: What is, is. Number two: What isn't, isn't."
The mystic continued: "A lot of people waste their time
focusing on what isn't—they dwell on things that aren't
real. If something's real, if it actually is—whether it's a feeling like anger or a fact like sales are down—it's a waste of
time wishing it wasn't. What you do if something is real is
accept it like it is, then decide if you want to put the energy
into
trying to make it different. Once you decide you want to try
to change it, then put your energy into what needs to be
done. That's everything you really need to be successful in
business and in life."
—GAY HENDRICKS and KATE LUDEMAN, *The Corporate Mystic*

life can be very complicated, and often when we are in the midst of challenging situations we can make things even more complicated by going over and over the possibilities. In our desperation to find an explanation for events as they happen we seek answers from friends, family, spiritual advisers, books, psychologists, and many other sources. Often such a search can leave us more confused than we were when we began.

When things don't turn out the way we want them to, it can be very difficult to accept. We can try to find a way of explaining away the things that we don't like and of clinging to the possibility that things will come around to our view. We can sit quietly and tell ourselves that everything will be all right if that person will just change their mind about things, or if that business deal will miraculously come out right, or if that friend or lover will just change their behavior, or if . . . or if . . . or if . . .

But you can't fight the world.

As the previous quote says, something either is or isn't. If you sit and dwell on the "if onlys," you confine yourself to wishing for a miracle. By spending all of your time focusing on the things that haven't worked out right, you use all of the energy that you need here in the present.

Have you been in this situation? Maybe something has happened that you really had a hard time accepting—a boyfriend or girlfriend dumped you, your 125th job application was rejected, a business deal went bad, your manuscript was rejected by the 34th publisher in succession. Did you sit in bed and cry your eyes out, go to the pub and get blind drunk, have an argument with your partner, scream at the dog, throw a tantrum?

I have.

I think we all like to believe that we are in total control. We don't like to let go of our fixed view of the world and the way we think things should turn out. To do so is akin to letting go of a child of our creative mind. To recover we must go through the grieving process of denial, resistance, anger, depression, and acceptance.

Until we can get to the stage of acceptance, our minds will be troubled. Depending on how tightly we wish to cling to the "if onlys," we can be stuck in any of the stages for a very long time.

The way to move forward is to let go of the way WE want things to be, and this is where faith becomes all-important. Faith allows us to move beyond the rational mind that endlessly tries to "work things out." Faith allows us to release ourselves from the oppressive belief that it is all up to us. Faith allows us to let go of the need to understand everything as it happens.

But the only way to get there is to let go of control.

If you are standing on the edge of the abyss wondering whether to leap and you bother to take a look around, you will see there are a whole lot of people there pottering about, muttering to themselves, and procrastinating. The first thing you want to say to them is, "Stop wasting time and leap!"

So why not you, too?

YES, it is simple. . . . Let go of the fear, let go of the doubt, let go of the anxiety. Have faith that life has meaning, have faith in yourself as a cocreator in the Universe. Put positive intent out there into the morphic field. Most importantly, have faith in human nature and our ability to collectively create a better world.

Ultimately it is up to you to save yourself from your fears, nobody else can do it for you.

But it is up to YOU to decide!

We need you.

a final word

I hope this book has been of some help to you. Thank you for being part of my journey, and I wish you courage and happiness on yours! Most of all, I want you to know that I BELIEVE IN YOU!!!!

> And if I have prophetic powers
> and understand all mysteries
> and all knowledge,
> and if I have faith,
> so as to move mountains,
> but I have not love,
> I am nothing.
> —I CORINTHIANS 13:2